THE

ROMANTIC IDEOLOGY

The
Romantic Ideology

A Critical Investigation

Jerome J. McGann

The University of Chicago Press

Chicago and London

THE UNIVERSITY OF CHICAGO PRESS, CHICAGO 60637
THE UNIVERSITY OF CHICAGO PRESS, LTD., LONDON
© 1983 by The University of Chicago
All rights reserved. Published 1983
Paperback edition 1985
Printed in the United States of America
04 03 02 01 00 99   6 7 8 9

Library of Congress Cataloging in Publication Data

McGann, Jerome J.
  The romantic ideology.

  Includes bibliographical references and index.
  1. English poetry—19th century—History and
criticism. 2. Romanticism. I. Title.
PR590.M34   1983   821'.7'09145   82-17494
ISBN 0-226-55850-9 (paper)

♾ The paper used in this publication meets the minimum
requirements of the American National Standard for
Information Sciences—Permanence of Paper for Printed
Library Materials, ANSI Z39.48-1984.

This book is dedicated
to my students at the University of Chicago,
1966–1975,
who taught me how to learn.

The only portions that were not consumed were some fragments of bones, the jaw, the skull, but what surprised us all, was that the heart remained entire. In snatching this relic from the fiery furnace, my hand was severely burnt; and had anyone seen me do the act I should have been put into quarantine.

E. J. Trelawny on Shelley's cremation

Contents

Preface

A few words must be said about the form and procedures of this book. Its explicit topics are Romantic poetry and Romantic criticism as these cultural products have continued to reproduce themselves, largely through academic discourse. The book does not attempt a comprehensive critical treatment of those topics, however, because it has been conceived in terms of a different (and somewhat larger) context. My aim has been to write a study of Romantic poetry and Romantic criticism insofar as these phenomena have sought to define themselves to and within post-Romantic culture at large. The book therefore rests on a crucial and unargued assumption: that western cultural history since 1789 is richer and more diverse than its various Romantic characterizations, and that those Romantic characterizations—both artistic and critical—can be usefully studied by placing them in a critical context which attempts to understand them in terms other than their own self-definitions.

Behind this book lies a sequence of essays which I have recently written, some of which have already appeared in print while others are soon to appear. All of these essays take up certain aspects of the theory and method of historical criticism. They are related to this book, and may help to fill out its larger critical context, by virtue of their being part of a general argument: that artistic products, whatever they may be formally, are materially and existentially social, concrete, and unique. Consequently, the study of such products must be carried out through a socio-historical framework which equally takes into account the human history of criticism and scholarship—those media by which culture maintains and reproduces the works which it inherits from the past. Furthermore, this book is being published at approximately the same time as another work, *A Critique of Modern Textual Criticism*, where I have tried to engage an historical criticism with the most fundamental area of all literary studies: textual criticism. This body of work comprises the initial parts of a comprehensive project which seeks to explain and restore an historical methodology to literary studies.

The personal aspects of the present work require a brief comment, especially since such a work may appear oddly described as part of a general project in historical method. But the historical focus in this book is not provided by its originary

Romantic materials; it comes from the context in which those materials were mediated and defined for me. This book is "about" Romanticism, that is to say, because my career as a scholar has been most heavily engaged with Romanticism and its scholarship. Had I been trained as a Restoration or Medieval scholar, the topics of this book would have been drawn from the Restoration or Medieval field. Consequently, this book might best be read as a critical meditation on the recent history of Romantic scholarship insofar as that history may provide an example, or perhaps a case study, of how literary criticism is involved with ideology, and how it might find the means for achieving a critical distance, however provisional, from its own ideological investments.

The dedication to this book acknowledges the deepest and most long-standing scholarly debt I have ever had, and one which I have not yet been able to acknowledge—only because of my own failure to see, until recently, just how deep that debt has been. Here I would like to name just one of those people, *pars pro toto*: Foster Chanock.

Introduction

The subject of the present book is the ideology of the Romantic tradition as it appears in the literary work in the early nineteenth century in England (the so-called Romantic Period). My interest in this subject grows out of my academic work, and in particular out of a desire to arrest a process which I have observed in my immediate experience as well as in the scholarly traditions which have helped to shape that experience. That is to say, the present work proposes a new, *critical* view of Romanticism and its literary products. To realize this aim necessitates an initial critique of the scholarly and critical traditions which have delivered these subjects into our hands. The ground thesis of this study is that the scholarship and criticism of Romanticism and its works are dominated by a Romantic Ideology, by an uncritical absorption in Romanticism's own self-representations.

To argue this position I have found it useful, perhaps even necessary, to study and emulate the critical procedures developed by Heine and, in general, to retrace many of the lines of inquiry which were first taken up in critical traditions we now associate with Marx. These traditions are useful, from a scholarly perspective, for two reasons. First, because they facilitate a critical analysis of the thought of clerics and academicians, they prove especially helpful to a clerical and academic mind like my own when it seeks to understand its formative ideas. Second, the socio-historical focus of Marxist criticism is an aid in elucidating the actual work of Romantic artists. The poetry of Romanticism is everywhere marked by extreme forms of displacement and poetic conceptualization whereby the actual human issues with which the poetry is concerned are resituated in a variety of idealized localities. A socio-historical method pursued within the Critical tradition helps to expose these dramas of displacement and idealization without, at the same time, debunking or deconstructing the actual works themselves.

It is the aim of this study to bring critique to the Ideology of Romanticism and its clerical preservers and transmitters, and to bring a measure of exposition to the works of the Romantic poets. These works are deeply involved with and affected by the ideologies of Romanticism, and they have even been used, by the priests and clerics of Romanticism (in whose number I am included), to perpetuate those ideologies. My own view—it follows Heine—is that Romantic poetry incorporates Romantic Ideology as a drama of the contradictions which are inherent to that ideology. In this respect Romantic poetry occupies an implicit—sometimes even an explicit—critical position toward its subject matter. The works of Romantic art, like the works of any historical moment, "transcend" their particular socio-historical position only because they are completely incorporated to that position, only because they have localized themselves. In this fact we observe that paradox fundamental to all works of art which is best revealed through an historical method of criticism: that such works transcend their age and speak to alien cultures because they are so completely true to themselves, because they are time and place specific, because they are—from our point of view—*different*.

Works of the past are relevant in the present, it seems to me, precisely because of this difference. We do not contribute to the improvement of social conditions or even to the advancement of learning—insofar as scholars improve or advance anything outside the field of scholarship—by seeking to erase this difference, but rather by seeking to clarify and promote it. When critics perpetuate and maintain older ideas and attitudes in continuities and processive traditions they typically serve only the most reactionary purposes of their societies, though they may not be aware of this; for the cooptive powers of a vigorous culture like our own are very great. If such powers and their results are not always to be deplored, cooptation must always be a process intolerable to a critical consciousness, whose first obligation is to resist incorporation, and whose weapon is analysis.

This is why the past and its works should be studied by a critical mind in the full range of their pastness—in their differences and their alienations (both contemporary and historical). To foster such a view of past works of art can only serve to increase our admiration for their special achievements and our sympathy for what they created within the limits which constrained them—as it were, for their grace under pressure.

Were this book concerned with contemporary literary products (say, the poems of James Merrill), its procedures would be quite different, necessarily. Brecht's argument with Lukács over the value of Modernism and its works[1] helps to clarify the essential difference which separates the journalistic and polemical criticism whose focus is the present from the scholarly and historical criticism which operates in the present only by facing (and defining) the past. These are two distinct types of criticism which ought not to be confused in practice. Such a confusion, it seems to me, has been too much a part of the academic criticism of our past literature for too long a time. This is particularly the case with the academic criticism of Romanticism, whose ideology continues to be translated and promoted, and whose works continue to be taught and valued for that ideology. I have tried in this book to arrest that process of reification: on the one hand, to situate Romanticism and its works in the past in order to make them present resources by virtue of their differential; and, on the other, to free present criticism from the crippling illusion that such a past establishes the limits, conceptual and practical, of our present and our future.

II

These critical remarks lead me to the second part of this Introduction, where I want to state, as succinctly as possible, some of the basic premises of this study, to provide descriptions of certain important and problematical terms, and finally to present my own view of how this book asks to be read.

This work assumes that poems are social and historical products and that the critical study of such products must be grounded in a socio-historical analytic. This does not mean that "purely" stylistic, rhetorical, formal, or other specialized analyses cannot or will not be pursued. Quite the contrary, as many of the sections of this book will go to show. What it does mean is that all such specialized studies must find their *raison d'être* in the socio-historical ground.

At this ground I assume that social functions are complex hierarchies made up of three interrelated levels: the political, the economic, and the ideological.[2] Poetry and literary criticism are products at the ideological level, where a culture's ideas and self-representations are maintained. Since I am principally concerned in this book with those ideological products we call works of literature, I want to be as explicit as possible about my understanding of the (deeply problematic) concept of ideology, as well as my view of its relevance to the works of Romanticism (both poetic and scholarly). Let me begin by turning to Coleridge, whose ideas on these topics are trenchant and, in

3

certain respects, normative to this day in certain lines of critical thought.

Toward the beginning of *The Statesman's Manual* (1816) Coleridge extols the biblical scribes and poets because they understood the necessary interdependence of knowledge and belief. In this respect they seemed to differ sharply from Enlightenment minds like Hume's, whose skeptical and rational methods Coleridge deplored.

> This inadequacy of the mere understanding to the apprehension of moral greatness we may trace in this historian's cool systematic attempt to steal away every feeling of reverence for every great name by a scheme of *motives*, in which as often as possible the efforts and enterprizes of heroic spirits are attributed to this or that paltry view of the most despicable selfishness. But in the majority of instances this would have been too palpably false and slanderous: and therefore the founders and martyrs of our church and constitution, of our civil and religious liberty, are represented as fanatics and bewildered enthusiasts. But histories incomparably more authentic than Mr. Hume's, (nay, spite of himself even his own history) confirm by irrefragable evidence the aphorism of ancient wisdom, that nothing great was ever achieved without enthusiasm. For what is enthusiasm but the oblivion and swallowing up of self in an object dearer than self, or in an idea more vivid?—How this is produced in the enthusiasm of wickedness, I have explained in the third Comment annexed to this Discourse. But in the genuine enthusiasm of morals, religion, and patriotism, this enlargement and elevation of the soul above its mere self attest the presence, and accompany the intuition of ultimate principles alone.[3]

"Every principle," Coleridge goes on to say, "is actualized by an idea, and every idea is living, productive . . . and . . . containeth an endless power of semination."[4] The human quest for knowledge and understanding had to bring—as Coleridge elsewhere said—"the whole soul of man into activity," and this involved the enthusiastic and *interested* pursuit of truth.

> And in nothing is Scriptual history more strongly contrasted with the histories of highest note in the present

age than in its freedom from the hollowness of abstractions. While the latter present a shadow-fight of Things and Quantities, the former gives us the history of Men, and balances the important influences of individual Minds with the previous state of the national morals and manners, in which, as constituting a specific susceptibility, it presents to us the true cause both of the Influence itself, and of the Weal or Woe that were its Consequents. How should it be otherwise? The histories and political economy of the present and preceding century partake in the general contagion of its mechanic philosophy, and are the *product* of an unenlivened generalizing Understanding.[5]

Coleridge's position is a defense of what we would now call "ideology," that is, a coherent or loosely organized set of ideas which is the expression of the special interests of some class or social group. Marx and the Marxist tradition would later identify the field of class interest as fundamentally economic, and would represent the social structure of Coleridge's "whole soul of man" as an interdependence of superstructure and infrastructure. A further difference between the Marxian and the Coleridgean analysis lies in the Marxist identification of Coleridge's "belief" and "enthusiasm" (along with the associated ideas or "contents") as a nexus of "false consciousness" which it was imperative to criticize and explore. From a Marxist perspective, Coleridge's views are praiseworthy in so far as they argue that knowledge is a social rather than an abstract pursuit. But because his position is a conceptual-idealist defense of Church, State, and the class interests which those institutions support and defend, Coleridge's ideas are, in a Marxist view, clearly deplorable.

Coleridge's views developed out of his revisionist study of that Enlightenment movement which centered in the historical study of classical and biblical texts. Because historical criticism had placed the authenticity of the Bible in peril, Coleridge sought (and found) a means for turning the new methods to the benefit of religion and the Church. He did so by arguing that the Bible contained a record of actual human belief, an image of God's people as they lived their faith, a drama of the progress of religious history.

In addition to this, the Hebrew legislator, and the other inspired poets, prophets, historians and moralists of the Jewish church have two immense advantages in their favor. First, their particular rules and prescripts flow directly and visibly from universal principles, as from a fountain: they flow from principles and ideas that are not so properly said to be confirmed by reason as to be reason itself! Principles, in act and procession, disjoined from which, and from the emotions that inevitably accompany the actual intuition of their truth, the widest maxims of prudence are like arms without hearts, muscles without nerves. Secondly, from the very nature of these principles, as taught in the Bible, they are understood in exact proportion as they are believed and felt. The regulator is never separated from the main spring. For the words of the apostle are literally and philosophically true: we (that is, the human race) live by faith. Whatever we do or know, that in kind is different from the brute creation, has its origin in a determination of the reason to have faith and trust in itself.[6]

Thus were the biblical texts and their stories saved from the merciless analytic probings of historical scholarship. These were not primitive documents containing the abstract ideas and precepts of some rationalistic system. Rather, they were ideas and principles "in act and procession," imbedded in particular social and historical circumstances. Errors, superstitions, and old-fashioned or positively anachronistic ideas and attitudes should therefore be no cause for alarm to the present-day Christian. Such things were to be expected in the course of God's relations with the history-bound peoples of His world. Ideas and the forms of faith changed with time and circumstances. The function of the true Higher Criticism was to trace out this organic historical development and raise it up in an act of higher consciousness.

My system, if I may venture to give it so fine a name, is the only attempt I know, ever made to reduce all knowledges into harmony. It opposes no other system, but shows what was true in each; and how that which was true in the particular, in each of them became error, *because* it was only half the truth. I have endeavored to unite the insulated fragments of truth, and therewith to frame a perfect mirror. I show to each system that I fully understand and rightly appreciate what that system means; but then I lift up that system to a higher point of view, from which I enable it to see its former position, where it was, indeed, but under another light and with different relations; so that the fragment of truth is not only acknowledged, but explained. Thus the old astronomers discovered and maintained much that was true; but, because they were placed on a false ground, and looked from a wrong point of view, they never did, and never could, discover the truth—that is, the whole truth. As soon as they left the earth, their false centre, and took their stand in the sun, immediately they saw the whole system in its true light, and their former station remaining, but remaining as a part of the prospect. I wish, in short, to connect by a moral *copula* natural history with political history; or, in other words, to make history scientific, and science historical—to take from history its accidentality, and from science its fatalism.[7]

Coleridge's views were to enjoy a truly remarkable triumph in England and America for one hundred and fifty years, particularly in those *petit bourgeois* enclaves which Coleridge called "the clerisy," that body of culture-guardians whose center today is in the academies. From Mill and Arnold to Mannheim, Trilling, and their successors, theories of ideology were reproduced which can be traced back to the models developed by Coleridge (and his German counterpart Hegel). In this line of analysis, ideology is marked by "false consciousness" and "error" because ideas are time and place specific and hence represent, in their successive points of view, "insulated fragments of truth." To understand the historicity of knowledge and belief is to have a higher self-conscious grasp of one's received intellectual traditions.

In Coleridge's critique of the Enlightenment he did not call his antagonists "ideologues" or their imputed abstract reasonings "ideology," but others who followed his or similar lines of approach did exactly that. Thus Scott refers to Napoleon's attacks upon that circle of late *philosophes* known as the Ideologues (after the term *idéologie* invented by Destutt de Tracy to denominate his science of ideas): "ideology, by which nickname the French ruler used to distinguish every species of theory . . .

7

resting in no respect upon a basis of self-interest." Like Coleridge, Napoleon condemned the ideologues and their science of ideas because it was analytic and abstract.

> It is to the doctrine of the ideologues—to this diffuse metaphysics, which in a contrived manner seeks to find the primary causes and on this foundation would erect the legislation of peoples, instead of adapting the laws to a knowledge of the human heart and of the lessons of history—to which one must attribute all the misfortunes which have befallen our beautiful France.[8]

This (Romantic and historicist) line of attack was soon to come under fire in its own right. That "higher point of view" which Coleridge occupied would be the cherished goal of Hegel and the left-wing Neo-Hegelians after him. Marx would call their position and ideas the German Ideology to distinguish it from the original French Ideology associated with Destutt de Tracy. Where French Ideology was critical, anti-religious, rational, and socially progressive, the German was synthetic, fideistic, speculative, and supportive of established power. In Hegel this was explicitly the case, but Marx argued that the position of the Neo-Hegelians was not fundamentally different. Marx's rationalistic and critical mind opened a broad-ranging attack upon this revisionist type of ideology in his great work *The German Ideology* (1845-7).

The German Ideology, Marx argued, characterizes its ideas as progressive and professes to seek an increase in consciousness. In fact, however, this German Ideology was based upon (and productive of) a false consciousness which insinuated an upside-down view of the world's realities. "Its active, conceptive ideologists," Marx says, "make the formation of the illusions of the [ruling] class about itself their chief source of livelihood."[9] That is to say, the German Ideologue presents an image of organic society and processive history—he offers a historicity and a sociology of ideas—because such an ideology helps to maintain the status quo and to conceal the truth about social relations: that the rich and the ruling classes dominate the poor and the exploited. A German Ideology serves the interests of the ruling classes, the State, the Church, and its ideologues. It is a system of illusions whose first dupes, according to Engels, are those very intellectuals who elaborate the system.

Ideology is a process which is indeed accomplished consciously by the so-called thinker, but it is the wrong kind of consciousness. The real motive forces impelling him remain unknown to the thinker; otherwise it simply would not be an ideological process. Hence he imagines false or illusory motive forces. Because it is a process of thinking he derives its form as well as its content from pure reasoning, either his own or that of his predecessors. He works exclusively with thought material, which he accepts without examination as something produced by reasoning, and does not investigate further for a more remote source independent of reason; indeed this is a matter of course to him, because, as all action is *mediated* by thought, it appears to him to be ultimately *based* upon thought.[10]

The source of this false consciousness, from a philosophical point of view, is in its conceptual basis. A German Ideology turns the world upside down and sees it from a false vantage because its own point of reference is conceptualized within a closed idealistic system.

Once the ruling ideas have been separated from the ruling individuals and, above all, from the relations which result from a given stage of the mode of production, and in this way the conclusion has been reached that history is always under the sway of ideas, it is very easy to abstract from these various ideas "the Idea," the thought, etc., as the dominant force in history, and thus to consider all these separate ideas and concepts as "forms of self-determination" of the Concept developing in history. It follows then, naturally, too that all the relations of men can be derived from the concept of man, man as conceived, the essence of man, Man. This has been done by speculative philosophy. Hegel himself confesses at the end of the *Geschichtsphilosophie* that he "has considered the progress of *the concept* only" and has represented in history the "true *theodicy*.". . . Now one can go back again to the producers of "the concept," to the theorists, ideologists and philosophers, and one comes then to the conclusion that the philosophers, the thinkers as such, have at all times been dominant in history: a conclusion, as we see, already expressed by Hegel.[11]

9

Or, we might well add, by Coleridge. According to Engels, this German Ideology is an

> occupation with thoughts as with independent entities, developing independently and subject only to their own laws. That the material life-conditions of the persons inside whose heads this thought process goes on in the last resort determines the course of this process remains of necessity unknown to these persons, for otherwise there would be an end to all ideology.[12]

When the term ideology is employed today its meaning derives ultimately from one of these three traditions: the Enlightenment tradition (or French Ideology, whose imputed rationalism is the sign that its historical consciousness is oriented almost exclusively in the present); the Romantic tradition (or German Ideology, characterized originally by a powerful historicism and an orientation toward the past as the locus of the secrets of historical process); the Critical tradition (or the Marxist view of ideology, which is a revisionary meditation on the previous two with an historical consciousness oriented toward change and the future). The French tradition is principally an analytic one and is most notable for its methodological and procedural rigor (the English counterpart of Destutt de Tracy and his circle is known as Benthamism). The Romantic tradition is principally a synthetic program whose center has been shifted from rational inquiry to imaginative pursuit (so-called "Speculative Philosophy"). The Critical tradition is, like the French, analytic and rational in its procedures, but it differs sharply from the Enlightenment tradition in that it takes history rather than ideas for its subject matter, and also because it is action-oriented (a Philosophy of Praxis).

III

This schematized history of the early formative concepts of ideology sets the terms in which the following discussions will take place. In the course of the book I generally prefer the term "ideology of poetry" to "theory of poetry" in order to emphasize the broad social and cultural determinations which are involved in the assumption of an intellectual position, particularly in the period when the concept of ideology was born. Furthermore, my point of view is consciously placed in what I have called the Critical tradition, and I have chosen Heine as my model for an actual practise of literary analysis. This choice has been dictated by two factors which have an important relation to my own position as a literary scholar. First, Heine was himself deeply involved with and sympathetic toward the literary works he criticized so trenchantly in *Die romantische Schule*. Second, even as he subjected the Romantic School to a severe critique of its ideology and ideological products, he also provided Romanticism with living quarters in a non-Romantic age and consciousness. Heine's critique of Romanticism sees its ideology as historically removed, as a consciousness with which Heine can no longer identify. But Heine's view *situates* Romanticism in the past, it does not *dismiss* it to the past. The difference here is important, for Heine's procedure offers (later) criticism a model and a program by which the historical resources of culture may continue to live and move and have their being in the present even as they are also recognized to be definitively placed in the past.

The artistic reproduction of ideology in literary works has this general effect: it historicizes the ideological materials, gives a local habitation and a name to various kinds of abstractions. When ideology thus acquires a human face, it draws the reader's consciousness to sympathy with the attitudes and forms of thought being advanced. A thematizing criticism may step in at this point either to reproduce, or to extend by transformation, the initially proferred forms of thought. Both Coleridge and Hegel take this approach. Of course, another line of thematic criticism remains possible—one which aims to deconstruct the originary works into pure ideology. In each of these cases, however, thematic criticism sidesteps the concrete, human particulars of the originary works, either to reproduce them within currently acceptable ideological terms, or to translate them into currently unacceptable forms of thought. The latter maneuver—so frequent today—generally operates by reducing poetic works to a network of related themes and ideas—a condition of being which no artistic product can tolerate without loss of its soul.[13]

The critical line of thought epitomized by Heine differs from these other approaches because it refuses to set the ideological materials of poetry free from their concrete historical environments. In this respect Heine's criticism is the earliest in a long and often broken red line which has recently gained a new birth of freedom in English studies through the work of Raymond Williams, whose fidelity to this "forlorn hope" of the intelligence has been an inspiration to many. My own work, it should be said, lies as much in debt to Williams as to Heine, and specifically to Williams' famous concept "structures of feeling." Like Heine, Williams is an important critic partly because he understands the central place which historical and ideological facts occupy in the experience we call poetry and the products we call poems. Much of his strength as a critic lies in his ability to save those materials for poetry without at the same time transforming them into abstract or trans-historical ideas.

This context may help to situate the aims and procedures of this book. In my view ideology will necessarily be seen as false consciousness when observed from any *critical* vantage, and particularly from the point of view of a materialist and historical criticism. Since this book assumes that a critical vantage can and must be taken toward its subject, the ideology represented through Romantic works is *a fortiori* seen as a body of illusions. Of course, from the vantage of its own self-representation an ideology is a complex form of consciousness which is more or less widely ramified through society—politically, culturally, and economically, and at the individual as well as the institutional level. A criticism which proceeds from within the ideology can at best see these structures as incomplete forms of consciousness—which is essentially the Coleridgean position. In literary criticism his line of inquiry is important, along with its German counterpart, Hegel's, because it set the terms of academic study which have been dominant ever since, but especially in the twentieth century.

Some Marxist critics, like Althusser, would like to separate poetry and art from ideology.[14] My own view is that this is a misguided effort which conceals a latent idealism. I take it that poetry, including Romantic poetry, "reflects"—and reflects upon—those individual and social forms of human life which are available to the artist's observation, and which are themselves a part of his process of observation. In the Romantic Period this double act of reflection—the representation and the self-conscious return—tends to situate the field of Romantic poetry at the ideological level in a specific way. One of the basic illusions of Romantic Ideology is that only a poet and his works can transcend a corrupting appropriation by "the world" of politics and money. Romantic poetry "argues" this (and other) illusions repeatedly, and in the process it "suffers" the contradictions of its own illusions and the arguments it makes for them. The readers of such works can benefit from them by turning this experiential and *aesthetic* level of understanding into a self-conscious and critical one.

The benefits to be gained from such an approach are two-fold. First, it opens to us an avenue of escape from certain illusions which we inherit and cherish from the past. When forms of thought enter our consciousness as forms (or "structures") of feeling—which is what takes place through poetry and art—the forms threaten to reify as ideology in the secondary environment of criticism. A critical procedure like Heine's undermines an ideological and reifying criticism by isolating and historicizing the originary forms of thought, by placing an intellectual gulf between the present and the past. At the same time Heine insists upon reproducing the concrete and human environment within which the ideologies of the past developed. This determination reveals the second advantage of such a criticism: the abstractions and ideologies of the present are thereby laid open to critique from another human world, and one which—by the privilege of its historical backwardness, as it were—can know nothing of our current historical illusions. Our own forms of thought thereby begin to enter our consciousness via the critique developed out of certain past forms of feeling. Like Trelawney at the cremation of Shelley, we shall reach for the unconsumed heart of the poem only if we are prepared to suffer a genuine change through its possession. Poetry is not to be had in the easy forms of our current ideologies.

This book conceives that our present culture has advanced, for better and for worse, well beyond those forms of consciousness which came to dominance in the Romantic Period and which are the subject of this study. At the same time, the critical representation of those forms of consciousness in our ideological apparatuses continues to suggest the opposite. Consequently, this book requests to be read at all times with a double awareness: of the actual differentials—political, economic, ideological—which separate the Romantic Period from our own, as well as of the persistent illusions that these differentials do not exist. Such illusions operate in the British and the American academies alike, though for rather different historical reasons. For the purposes of the present study these differences will not be taken up, since they seem to me to ask for a separate historical inquiry of their own.

One final word by way of introduction. In the course of this study I shall often be recalling the critical power which past works of poetry exercise on present acts of reading and criticism. Since my specific subject is Romantic poetry, my general point is open to an interpretive ambiguity. Let me state here, then, that while I shall be arguing for the critical resources of Romantic poetry in particular, my general position would go further to suggest that all inherited works of literature have it in their power to force a critical engagement with any present form of thought (whether a critical or an ideological form) by virtue of the historical differentials which separate every present from all the past—by virtue of those differentials which draw the present and the past together across the field of concrete and particular differences.

PART I

Romanticism
and Its
Critical Representations

1

Distinguishing Romanticism

What we have come to call Romanticism in literature was a movement born in an era marked by radical sets of conflicts and contradictions. Later scholars and critics who have labored to define and understand these phenomena have, not unexpectedly, turned up a mare's nest of problems. The extremity of these discussions seemed to be reached in the positions taken by Lovejoy, on the one hand, and Wellek on the other. Both argued that Romanticism (whether "intrinsic" or historical) comprised a vast and heterogeneous body of material; but where Wellek saw a basic unity in that diversity, Lovejoy argued that critical rigor permitted nothing less precise than a careful "discrimination of Romanticisms."[1]

The difference of opinion separating Wellek and Lovejoy merely epitomizes the general terms in which critics had been discussing the problem of Romanticism for decades. That is to say, Wellek and Lovejoy joined with each other on commonly accepted ground. When Lovejoy surveys the critical discussions of Romanticism, he does not dismiss the received conclusions of the critics and scholars. On the contrary, his despair arises precisely because he finds himself persuaded by the received scholarship, whose contradictions and differentials seem so painfully apparent to him. Wellek, on the other hand, believes that the contradictions are only apparent, and that if the set of cultural phenomena called Romanticism is difficult to define, the problem is purely nominalistic. Wellek's argument is that scholars and critics all basically agree on what Romanticism is or was in *fact*, however much they may differ in their definitional terms and schemes. "The terms 'romantic' and 'romanticism'," he says, have always and everywhere been "understood in approximately the same sense," and hence are "still useful as terms for the kind of literature produced after neoclassicism." Wellek proposes his own analytic for such terms, but his "three criteria" are offered in a diplomatic and modest spirit. Their comprehensiveness lies not so much in their analytic rigor as in the widespread acceptability of Wellek's formulation:

the following three criteria should be particularly convincing, since each is central for one aspect of the practice of literature: imagination for the view of poetry, nature for the view of the world, and symbol and myth for poetic style.[2]

Wellek's argument was made in 1949 and the subsequent critical literature on Romanticism eloquently testifies to the triumph of his general position. Indeed, this result was inevitable since informed persons *do* generally agree on what is comprised under the terms Romantic and Romantic Movement. I do not mean to say by this that Lovejoy's arguments were not important. On the contrary, Lovejoy's position—which calls attention not so much to a problem in the phenomena being studied as to a crisis in the disciplines of investigation—assumes today, once again, a paramount significance. For if Lovejoy directed his essay into what he saw as a Babel of criticism, the present scholarly situation often appears so ignorant or forgetful of its subject, so intent upon its own productive process, that it seems capable of any sort of nonsense. This judgment is perhaps a severe one, especially for a person who—as the rest of this essay will show—has learned so much from recent criticism of Romanticism. I can only say that some severity seems called for since criticism has, of late, increasingly allowed its rigor and clarity—its scholarly obligations—to lapse in disuse.

Let me illustrate what I mean by some recent work in Jane Austen criticism. Taking proper note of the fact that "the place of Jane Austen in literary history" is a neglected and important subject, Gene Ruoff put together a series of essays on the relation of Austen to her period. These appeared in a special issue of *The Wordsworth Circle*.[3] As I have said, the general subject of these essays was and still is a crucial one, and while many of the pieces—but particularly those by Kestner and Ruoff—contain some important insights, the general approach fills one with dismay. For even as these writers correctly protest against "omitting Jane Austen from our general discussions of English Romanticism," almost all work on the assumption that the omission will be rectified if one can see and isolate the Romantic elements in Austen's work. A solution to a crucial problem in literary periodization is thus sought for by a simple rectifying proposition: Austen's relation to her period has been a neglected subject because traditional criticism has judged her as un- or non-Romantic. Austen is returned to her period by arguing the case of her Romanticism. The *ne plus ultra* of this argument emerged recently in an essay by Nina Auerbach which explicitly acknowledges its debt to *The Wordsworth Circle*'s symposium of essays. "Jane Austen and Imprisonment" draws its comparison between *Sense and Sensibility* and *Melmoth the Wanderer* on purely metaphoric grounds. The argument is that since "the ultimate prison is acquiescence," the critic may draw literary-historical parallels between a novel which focusses on the prisons of the Inquisition and a novel which focusses on a young woman submitting to inherited authority in the choice of a marriage partner. Auerbach's characterization of the force of each novel seems to me accurate; what one demurs at is the generic yoking of these works, the imputing of an ideological parallel between two very different sorts of novel on the basis of an idea (imprisonment) which is an originary and literal fact in one, but which is only a secondary and critical metaphor in the other.[4]

Misconceptions of these kinds are not in themselves very important. What is important, however, is the assumption made by so many of the critics who took up the subject of Jane Austen and Romanticism: that if Austen is not to be seen "either as a figure outside the bounds of literary history or as a throwback to an earlier time,"[5] then she must be seen as a Romantic. This assumption, I submit, is thoroughly misguided, and when critics work from it they have not only obscured the special historical significance of Austen's work, they confuse the entire subject of Romanticism both in its structural and its historical formations. Not every artistic production in the Romantic period is a Romantic one, as one might see at a glance from Hazlitt's *Spirit of the Age*; indeed, the greatest artists in any period often depart from their age's dominant ideological commitments, as the example of Austen so dramatically illustrates. The Romantic Age is so called not because all its works are Romantic, but rather because the ideologies of Romanticism exerted an increasingly dominant influence during that time.

To study the subject of Romanticism, then, particularly at this time, we can usefully begin by reminding ourselves that some writers and some works are not Romantic—even in the Romantic Period itself. Understanding this helps to distinguish the subject through a defining set of contrasts. Furthermore, a general analytic of differentiations—which Lovejoy pursued in his classic essay on Romanticism(s)—seems to me the most useful scholarly method that one could adopt at this juncture, because the critical literature on Romanticism has begun to lose its grip on the historical and structural peculiarities of Romantic works. If it used to be true, as Wellek has suggested, that critics generally agreed in their understanding of what is included under the term Romanticism, one would scarcely be able to tell this any longer from the more current scholarly literature on the subject. The triumph of Wellek's unified field theory has been such that the character of scholarly agreement is in danger of utter trivialization. Nowhere is this more apparent than in the now widespread idea that Romanticism comprises all significant literature produced between Blake and the present—some would say between Gray, or even Milton, and the present.

This will never do. Let me begin to reopen the problem of defining Romanticism, then, by examining some significant critical commentaries. I take it that Wellek and Lovejoy have set the terms of the critical discussion. In what follows I will start with some recent commentaries which help locate the fault lines that have developed in recent criticism. I will then retreat to take up the chief theoretical vantages under which the Romantic Movement was delivered over as a subject to later ages. Here I will be suggesting that three general approaches to the subject dominate the field, and that these were epitomized in the work of Coleridge, Hegel, and Heine.

Distinguishing these three approaches will enable us, finally, not only to understand better the critical history of Romanticism, but to approach the actual works of the Romantic Movement with greater precision and clarity. In Parts II and III of this study such a closer approach will be essayed: first, to distinguish some of the salient characteristics of Romantic poetry *per se*; and second, to submit this poetry to a critique which clarifies the limits of Romantic poetry and its ideologies. The study concludes by drawing attention to some larger matters that have to do with the study of poetry in general, and with certain current critical practices in particular.

2

Some Current Problems

in Literary Criticism

In a recent, interesting discussion of "The Paradigm of Romantic Irony," Anne Mellor proposes to offer a corrective to Meyer
Abrams' famous thesis, set forth in *Natural Supernaturalism*,
that the model for Romantic art can be found "in the secular-
ized Judaeo-Christian traditions."[6] What Mellor offers is another
model based on the "theory of Romantic irony":

> the authentic romantic ironist is as filled with
> enthusiasm as with skepticism. He is as much a roman-
> tic as an ironist. Having ironically acknowledged the
> fictiveness of his own patternings of human experience,
> he romantically engages in the creative process of life by
> eagerly constructing new forms, new myths. And these
> new fictions and self-concepts bear with them the seeds
> of their own destruction. They too die to give way to
> new patterns, in a never-ending process that becomes an
> analogue for life itself. The resultant artistic mode that
> alone can properly be called romantic irony must there-
> fore be a form or structure that simultaneously creates
> and de-creates itself.[7]

This dialectical model is Mellor's alternative to Abrams' "conception of an ordered, teleological universe" which Mellor finds
deficient in its failure to take account of Romantic skepticism.
The latter is necessary to Mellor's view of the Romantic program of "creative process" because irony permits the Romantic
artist to "deconstruct his mystifications of the self and the world"
and thus to renew forever his "contact with a greater creative
power."[8]

As Mellor insists later, however, the skeptical or ironic element in Romantic Irony should not be used to shift "the emotional emphasis of Schlegel's concept from celebration to desperation." The latter is the shift pointed out in D. C. Meucke's now standard work,[9] whereas in Mellor's view "the romantic ironist's enthusiastic response to process and change terminates where the perception of a chaotic universe arouses either guilt or fear."[10] In Mellor's view, the emergence of either guilt or fear signals the termination of Romantic Irony and the beginning of "something else." Mellor does not tell us what begins at that critical point, nor does she suggest whether it is—or could be, or might be—a Romantic phenomenon. We must presume, since one of her examples is taken from Coleridge, that it could be Romantic, but since the other example is Lewis Carroll we might equally well judge that it need not be (though it might be). This surmise is borne out by Mellor's remarks about Abrams' critical formulations, which she takes to be accurate descriptions of at least some forms of Romantic art.

Mellor's engagement with Abrams over the issue of Romantic Irony begins to suggest how complicated the subject of Romanticism can be. At least three different "Romanticisms" are taken for granted in Mellor's remarks: one treated by Abrams (adequately, in Mellor's view); a second to be taken up by Mellor herself in her discussion of Romantic Irony; and a third (dark, sinister) variety hinted at in Mellor's references to Muecke's treatment of the issue of Romantic Irony. I shall refer to this type as Kierkegaard's, since he was the first to discuss and analyze it in detail.[11] Mellor's references to it are important because they serve to highlight the character of her general view of Romanticism, which presents a significant modification of Abrams' position rather than an alternative to it. At the heart of both lies an emphasis upon the "creative process" of Romanticism, both in its forms and in its dominant themes. Both critics emphasize what Mellor calls "celebration," or "an enthusiastic response to process and change." What Mellor seeks to do is broaden Abrams' basic categories so that they can be brought to include the "skeptical" and "ironic" productions of an artist like Byron, whom Abrams had difficulty accommodating to his scheme.

At this point, the differential which separates Abrams and Mellor on the one hand from Kierkegaard on the other begins to assume a troubling significance. What, we want to know, is the Romantic Irony which Kierkegaard has delineated—a type of Romanticism or, in Mellor's words, "something else"? Kierkegaard and Muecke after him both regard the phenomena as Romantic in character; indeed, their formulations constitute a special investigation in the field laid out by Mario Praz in *The Romantic Agony*. If we turn to Praz, then, we come upon a standard account of the nature of Romantic literary productions which contrasts sharply with the views of Abrams and Mellor:

> The word 'romantic' thus comes to be associated with another group of ideas, such as 'magic', 'suggestive', 'nostalgic', and above all with words expressing states of mind which cannot be described. . . . The essence of Romanticism consequently comes to consist in that which cannot be described. The word and the form, says Schlegel in *Lucinde*, are only accessories. The essential is the thought and the poetic image, and these are rendered possible only in a passive state. The Romantic exalts the artist who does not give a material form to his dreams—the poet ecstatic in front of a forever blank page, the musician who listens to the prodigious concerts of his soul without attempting to translate them into notes. It is romantic to consider concrete expression as a decadence, a contamination. How many times has the magic of the ineffable been celebrated, from Keats, with his
>
> > Heard melodies are sweet, but those unheard
> > Are sweeter . . . .
>
> to Maeterlinck, with his theory that silence is more musical than any sound![12]

Praz's remarks draw us back to a commonplace truth about Romantic works which some tend to forget, especially in these happy and upright days when so much emphasis is placed upon Romanticism as a "creative," "enthusiastic," and "celebratory" ideology: that numerous works widely acknowledged to be Romantic are nihilistic, desperate, and melancholy.[13]

So we return to our uncomfortable commonplaces. No one has to tell us that the Romanticism of "La Belle Dame Sans Merci," or *Don Juan*, Canto XI, differs sharply from that of "The Rime of the Ancient Mariner" or Book 6 of *The Prelude*.

Equally certain is the fact that "an enthusiastic response to process and change" will not characterize the melancholy of Keats's ballad or Byron's sad canto. Praz's Romantic Agony seems a more apposite paradigm for works of such a sort—for Coleridge's "Limbo," Wordsworth's great elegy on "Peele Castle," and for Shelley's fragmentary masterpiece "The Triumph of Life." Once again we have to confront the prospect of Lovejoy's Romanticisms rather than with Wellek's unified view.

I have focussed on Mellor's discussion not to set it apart for criticism, but to offer it as an instance of something we frequently encounter in contemporary scholarship. Commentators observe what appears to be the same subject matter and yet come away from it with conflicting representations of what they have seen. Sometimes this happens because the critic neglects to study all the data offered by his subject. Abrams is a good example here, for although he erects a comprehensive theory of Romanticism, it does not rest upon an investigation of Keats or, more crucially, of Byron. Mellor's work steps in precisely to call attention to this weakness in Abrams' theory and to rectify it. But Mellor's study raises new sets of problems, as we have seen. In her view, whatever forms do not show "an enthusiastic response to process and change" are "something else" than Romantic. Comprehensiveness is achieved by definitional exclusion.

This tendency to ignore or to gerrymander the phenomena to be studied is common in our disciplines. It springs from the laudable and necessary impulse to establish continuities between past literature and present cultural imperatives. Abrams and Mellor tell us a great deal about their own ideological commitments when they characterize their subject. "The great Romantic poems," Abrams has said, "were not written in the mood of revolutionary exaltation but in the later mood of revolutionary disillusionment and despair."[14] This is historically exact, but it leads Abrams to extend his remarks into some interesting, more polemical, and less historically accurate ways. These great Romantic poems, he goes on to say, "turn on the theme of hope and joy and the temptation to abandon all hope and fall into dejection and despair."[15] Reading this we suspect that he has more in mind certain works and certain poets than others, and the suspicion is borne out in Abrams' completed formulation:

Wordsworth evokes from the unbounded and hence impossible hopes in the French Revolution a central Romantic doctrine; one which reverses the cardinal neo-classic ideal of setting only accessible goals, by converting what had been man's tragic error—the inordinacy of his "pride" that persists in setting infinite aims for finite man—into his specific glory and his triumph. Wordsworth shares the recognition of his fellow-Romantics, German and English, of the greatness of man's infinite *Sehnsucht*, his saving insatiability, Blake's "I want! I want!" Shelley's "the desire of the moth for the star"; but with a characteristic and unique difference, as he goes on at once to reveal:

> Under such banners militant, the soul
> Seeks for no trophies, struggles for no spoils
> That may attest her prowess, blest in thoughts
> That are their own perfection and reward. . . .

The militancy of overt political action has been transformed into the paradox of spiritual quietism: under such militant banners is no march, but a wise passiveness. This truth having been revealed to him, Wordsworth at once goes on to his apocalypse of nature in the Simplon Pass, where the *coincidentia oppositorum* of its physical attributes become the symbols of the biblical Book of Revelation:

> Characters of the great Apocalypse,
> The types and symbols of Eternity,
> Of first, and last, and midst, and without end.

This and its companion passages in *The Prelude* enlighten the orphic darkness of Wordsworth's "Prospectus" for *The Recluse*, drafted as early as 1800, when *The Prelude* had not yet been differentiated from the larger poem. Wordsworth's aim, he there reveals, is still that of the earlier period of millennial hope in revolution, still expressed in a fusion of biblical and classical imagery. Evil is to be redeemed by a regained Paradise, or Elysium: "Paradise," he says, "and groves/ Elysian, Fortunate Fields . . . why should they be/ A history only of departed things?" And the restoration of Paradise, as in the Book of Revelation, is still symbolized by a sacred marriage. But the hope has been shifted from the

history of mankind to the mind of the single individual,
from militant external action to an imaginative act; and
the marriage between the Lamb and the New Jerusalem
has been converted into a marriage between subject and
object, mind and nature, which creates a new world out
of the old world of senses.[16]

The passage is from Abrams' great essay "English Romanticism:
The Spirit of the Age," which appeared in 1963. Here lies the
origin of what Harold Bloom would later call the Internalization
of Quest Romance.[17]

Abrams' deeply influential ideas are clearly drawn from a
Wordsworthian and, more generally, a Christian (Protestant)
model. Equally clear is that these ideas elide the problematic
cases of Keats and Byron, and that they propose a moral evalua-
tion of the "message" of "the great Romantic poems" as well as a
certain canonization of the phenomena. "Despair" is an emotional state to be shunned if not deplored, and it is associated
explicitly with "the unbounded and hence impossible hopes" of
political and social transformation. "Hope," on the other hand, is
a good thing, and it is associated with an "infinite *Sehnsucht*"
which is possible to achieve: that is, with a psychological victory,
a religious and spiritual success which can replace the failed
hope of social melioration.

Before anything else one must call attention to the paradox
which Abrams is proposing. On the one hand, social and political goals—hopes aimed at transformations in a mortal
continuum—are pronounced to be "impossible" and
"unbounded";[18] on the other hand, the *Sehnsucht* of Romanticism, which most early commentators associated with a nostalgic condition of Romantic Agony, is here moved into a relation
with what is possible, that is to say, with spiritual territories and
religious ideas. One is obliged to observe, of course, that such a
transcendental displacement of human desires is the basis of the
(formerly) common view that Romanticism was (and is) a reactionary movement. This is the displacement which Marx saw as
a drug on human consciousness. In philosophy it is called the
German Ideology.

Abrams' historical characterizations, then, are a function of
a certain ideology, and their persuasive force waxes and wanes
to the degree that we can agree to accept that ideology. Mellor

secularizes the model by introducing the element of Romantic skepticism, but she does so only to the point where such skepticism does not "turn from celebration to desperation." No agonies are allowed into her Romantic world which is, like Abrams', a good and happy place: a place of enthusiasm, creative process, celebration, and something evermore about to be.

But, as with Abrams, Mellor's presentation falls victim to the deeper critique announced by the subject matter itself—a critique which, as critics like Kierkegaard and Praz remind us, was and always will remain an essential and original feature of Romanticism itself. We remember "Peele Castle" and the later poems of Coleridge; and we have kept our Byron open and read as well the great and troubled works of Keats, and so many poems of Shelley's like "When the lamp is shattered." As Wellek would say, we know these to be deeply Romantic works, but they seem to fall outside these critics' abilities to account for them under their definitions of Romanticism.

Let me pause and summarize for a moment. What I have been saying so far takes its origin from Lovejoy's critical procedures. The examples I have used could easily be multiplied to show what Lovejoy, in a slightly different way, has already made plain: that definitions of Romanticism are legion because none exhaust the various elements which learned commentators have shown to be characteristic of the subject. Even Wellek, who has produced the most influential holistic view in our period, is not exempt from an argument-by-exception: the "three criteria" which he calls "central" to a Romantic "practice of literature" do not at all fit Byron, who is perhaps the single most important figure in the history of European Romanticism. I should add that Wellek's criteria are deeply problematic in themselves, for the uses of myth by Romantic artists are no more uniform than are their concepts of imagination or their attitudes toward nature. The criterion of myth encompasses a practice which extends from the now widely recognized mythopoeic approaches, which are fundamentally symbolistic, to the now largely forgotten mythographic procedures, which are basically allegorical in method.[19] Indeed, historically oriented scholars will understand that the latter were far more characteristic of Romantic practice than the former: mythopoeia does not fully emerge in English poetry until the later nineteenth century.

The example of Abrams helps us to see another characteristic of scholarly treatments of Romanticism: that the scholarship is everywhere informed by ideological commitments of various kinds. Let me hasten to add that such commitments do not in themselves vitiate a scholarship or criticism. All science and knowledge is pursued from a particular socio-historical vantage and hence embodies certain ideological presuppositions. The scholarship is weakened only to the degree that its point of view does not (perhaps it cannot) account for all the available data. It is in this area that a Lovejoyan argument-by-exception gains its force and authority, as we have seen. Equally important to see, however, is the *fact* of the presence of ideology. Seeing this enables us to define more precisely the special vantage of a criticism, and thereby to isolate some of the sources of its scholarly limits.

The presence of ideology in criticism is particularly difficult to see because the chief disciplines of cultural analysis are themselves vehicles for the production of ideology. In the contemporary world they are the chief means of production, and literary criticism is an important tool within the larger system. Literary criticism presents its results in finished and comprehensive forms, sometimes even in transcendental and non-historical forms. The reader must therefore be on his guard to demystify such works of their ideological self-representations if he is to be in a position to assess the adequacy of their assertions.

Lovejoy's methods, which are fundamentally phenomenological, will not serve to elucidate such matters. Historical criticism becomes more useful at this point since the failures of scholarship, in literary matters, frequently result from a lack of attention to historical differentials. We are, for example, accustomed nowadays to hear Romantic literature characterized as a "poetry of process" and to accept this sort of formulation without serious demur. But when we recall that the same term has been applied to the work of Pound and Charles Olson, and that a process model has been equally employed to explain Chaucer, Spenser, Milton, and Marvell, and to distinguish Medieval from Renaissance poetic methods, we recognize the poverty of such a concept when it is used to define some special quality in Romantic literature. Whatever else it involves—whatever its usefulness in various, often excellent, critical discussions—this idea cannot serve to *distinguish* the

28

literary phenomena of Romanticism.

Such loose critical thinking is more characteristic of our period than one likes to remember, as the initial example from Austen scholarship indicated. The work of Wellek, Lovejoy, and Praz seems all the more impressive by contrast. I want to give here one or two more examples which can serve as a transition to the next phase of my argument.

In a well-regarded book subtitled "Coleridge and the Romantic Tradition" J. Robert Barth sums up his view of Romantic poetry as a "poetry of encounter":

> Romanticism is often said to be marked by a new sense of freedom. This includes . . . a freedom that has not often been noted . . . that comes precisely from the symbolic experience. It is the freedom given the reader by the poet. Since we are simply led into the experience—are not told, as in allegory or other poetry of fancy, what to experience—we are left free to be, perhaps to find, ourselves.[20]

We can pass by without comment the facile, but very Coleridgean, view of allegory implicit in the passage, since it so patently misrepresents that genre. What interests me particularly is the "Reader-response" definition which Barth gives to Romanticism. His view is in fact fairly widespread but—once again—a scholarly mind must be dismayed by the lack of rigor in the argument. For what can be so specifically Romantic about such a poetic method if—as many others tell us—it is equally characteristic of Bacon, Milton, Bunyan (an allegorist!), and a host of other older and more recent writers?

Or, to return to Jane Austen, we may recall another recent essay which sought to demonstrate the Romanticism of her work. It is true, of course, that Jane Austen's work is at certain points influenced by Romanticism. But the critic did not mean to say this, or to specify how and where Romanticism appears in her (basically, quite un-Romantic) works. For this critic, Jane Austen could be seen as a sort of closet Romantic because a study of her work showed that she "harbored the subversive—and therefore Romantic—desire that women be trained to think rationally."[21] The problem with this statement is in the parenthetical assumption that a subversive idea is equivalent to a Romantic idea (either in itself, or perhaps with

29

the added qualification that the idea should belong to the "Romantic Period"). This assumption is quite wrong, and profoundly unhistorical. Many subversive ideas (even in the Romantic Period) are not at all Romantic ideas, and many Romantic ideas are by no means subversive. Only an historical analysis of the particular instances can decide such matters.

These various examples demonstrate the interested, partisan focus which critical argumentation will take. Austen is valued because she is a "subversive" writer and Romanticism is elevated for the same reason. For Barth, on the other hand, Romantic poetry is important for giving us "the terrible and beautiful freedom to encounter the mysteries of man." Mellor values Romanticism for its "creative process" and Abrams for its spirituality. As I have already noted, criticism must adopt an evaluative position of some sort toward itself and its subject matter; but it will vitiate its own activity to the extent that it has not shown a clear understanding of the symmetries and differences which hold between the critics' values on the one hand, and the (historically removed) subject on the other. Because the persuasive power of criticism rests ultimately on the rigor of its intellectual operations, its own judgments gain authority only when they are presented in a severe critical medium of their own. We may take it as a rule, then, that any criticism which abolishes the distance between its own (present) setting and its (removed) subject matter—any criticism which argues an unhistorical symmetry between the practicing critic and the descending work—will be, to that extent, undermined as criticism. In such cases criticism becomes important in the history of ideology rather than in the history of criticism.

Needless to say, I am not suggesting here that the ideological polemic of criticism should be sacrificed to a (spurious) critical objectivity, or vice versa. What I am saying is that no critical polemic will succeed, or will help to advance its total view, when it allows its discourse to operate at a relatively casual critical level. Personally I am more troubled by what one sees in recent Austen criticism than by the other examples brought forward here. This is so because many of the critics engaged with Austen are clearly wrestling with the more significant scholarly problems. The attempt to establish explicit connections between ideology and scholarship is a difficult but vitally important task, especially in Anglo-American scholarship where the illusion of objectivity continues to be pursued, whether hypocritically or in ignorance. But the importance of the work only places upon it a greater obligation to excellence. To speak of Austen as a "subversive" writer or of Romanticism as a subversive movement is to misuse words shamelessly, to violate the mind and encourage confusion of thought: the last result being, let me say, the mortal sin of every form of criticism. The ground of any critical polemic must finally come to rest upon its intellectual reliability. Without that fundamental initiation its programs of good intentions must in the end come to seem at best splendid adventures, and at worst mere houses built on sand.

3

Two Normative Theories of Romanticism

and Heine's Critique

This critical survey of a few important aspects of the scholarship of Romanticism during the past fifty years or so provides a necessary point of departure for a new examination of the subject. The fundamental argument between Wellek and Lovejoy—both scholars with acute and well-trained historical perceptions—reflects a paradox, or conflict, which has characterized Romanticism from its earliest self-representations. In *The Great Chain of Being* Lovejoy had no difficulty showing, from original Romantic documents, that Romanticism was a movement which attacked received ideas of uniformity, standardization, and universality with "the idealization of diversity," with a program which set the highest value upon the unique, the peculiar, the local: what Schlegel called "the abnormal species of literature . . . even the eccentric and monstrous." [22] Wellek, on the other hand, pursued his investigations under the influence of the integrative impulse present in the earliest programmatic Romantics. When Wellek says that "All Romantic poets conceived of nature as an organic whole, on the analogue of man rather than a concourse of atoms,"[23] his point of departure is a collection of central Romantic texts, not the least important of which is Coleridge's famous *rifacimento* of certain important German documents:

> The poet, described in *ideal* perfection, brings the whole soul of man into activity, with the subordination of its faculties to each other, according to their relative worth and dignity. He diffuses a tone, and spirit of unity, that blends, and (as it were) *fuses*, each into each, by that synthetic and magical power, to which we have exclusively appropriated the name of imagination. This power, first put in action by the will and understanding, and retained under their irremissive, though gentle and unnoticed controul . . . reveals itself in the balance or reconciliation of opposite or discordant qualities.[24]

The earliest comprehensive effort to reconcile this root conflict of impulses in Romanticism was made by Hegel in his "Introduction to the Philosophy of Art." This influential document argued that Romanticism, which is epitomized in the medium of poetry, represented a higher synthesis of two anterior forms of art: the Symbolic and the Classical. This contemplative and spiritual line—indeed, this late Christian view of art— underlies the approach taken by Abrams, as well as the many variants and derivatives which persist in contemporary criticism. Its force as criticism rests in its ability to reconcile conceptually that fundamental conflict of concepts which we have already noted in Romanticism and its scholarship alike.

The difficulty with such a view lies precisely in its conceptual and programmatic character. Like Hegel, Abrams offers a program of Romanticism rather than a critical representation of its character; as such, both reify certain key Romantic self-conceptualizations like "spirituality," "creativity," "process," "uniqueness," "diversity." Indeed, the concepts of "synthesis" and "reconciliation" as these appear in the received Romantic texts and their commentaries are themselves Romantic concepts whose meaning cannot be taken at face value. They lie at the very heart of Romanticism's self-representation and as such they must be subjected to critical analysis. This analysis is difficult to perform, however, since the ideologies of Romanticism seek to persuade us that such concepts are fundamental, and hence that they need not—cannot—be analyzed. Such an argument, which we should still call The German Ideology, was first criticized by Stendhal and Heine along cultural and political lines, but their method of analysis has fallen into disuse, in the academy especially. To understand Romanticism today, we should recall, and partly recover, their critical strategies.

In the field of cultural and literary studies the method is epitomized in Heine's classic essay *The Romantic School*, a work which I shall take up later in more detail.[25] Here I want only to discuss the general purposes, shape, and procedure of the essay. At its heart is Heine's commitment to intellectual freedom—and not merely to the abstract idea of such a freedom, but to the political and social acts which alone can make the idea a living reality. Equally crucial to see is that the essay is a polemic grounded in an historical analysis both of its subject—which is removed in time and circumstances—and of Heine's immediate audience. He writes between 1833 and 1835 as an expatriate German Jew to a French intellectual public about a cultural phenomenon, German Romanticism, which is now historically concluded. His French audience, of course, has only recently experienced the emergence of a new Romanticism in France. Heine's purpose is to provide his audience with some guidelines for understanding, and hence for using, the earlier German movement.

This structure of circumstances dictates the central preoccupations of the essay. At every point Heine is concerned with the problem of the immediate relevance of removed cultural resources—in this case, German Romantic literary works. He is qualified to take up this problematic matter because he contains within himself, as it were, a crucial division of sympathies and knowledge. The fact that he is a German living in France dramatizes a whole range of related dialectical symmetries. The root doubleness of Heine's critique is most apparent in the witty and ironic style of his famous essay. Critics have sometimes taken this style as a license for ignoring or overlooking the seriousness of Heine's critique. We must resist such a facile approach, however, since the importance of the essay lies exactly in its management of dialectics.

The critique is based on a whole series of related patterns of antithesis. The most important of these is the fact that Heine is a writer whose youthful allegiance had been connected with

German Romanticism, but whose literary commitments in 1833-5 have changed under the pressure of historical events. The relevance of Romanticism to Heine in 1833 is not what it was in 1813. The distance he has moved has introduced the possibility of a critical dialectic, in two ways: the cultural phenomena of the past can be invoked to place present culture under a contrastive analysis, and the perspective of immediate circumstances can release a critical judgment upon the works of the past. As a consequence, Heine produces all his judgments from a critical distance which itself always remains open to critique from a distance. His sympathy for the past—and hence the immediate relevance of the past—rests in Heine's insistence upon its continuous critical powers.

A brief example of the procedure must serve for the moment. Heine's essay is notorious for its attack upon the Neo-Catholic ideology of German Romanticism and the movement's generally escapist and reactionary character. A. W. Schlegel is the focussing point of Heine's remarks on these matters. But when Heine's polemical analysis turns its ironic attention to the present, the medievalism and escapist impulses of the Romantic School are provided with new opportunities.

> In the Middle Ages most people believed that when a building was to be erected, it was necessary to kill some living creature and lay the cornerstone on its blood; in this way the building would stand firm and indestructible. . . . Today mankind is more sensible. We no longer believe in the magic power of blood, either the blood of an aristocrat or a god, and the great masses believe only in money. . . .[P]eople. . . ascribe magic power only to minted metal, to the Host of silver and gold; money is the beginning and the end of all their works; and when they have a building to erect, they take great pains to see that some coins, a capsule with all kinds of coins, is placed under the cornerstone.
>
> Yes, as in the Middle Ages everything, single buildings as well as the whole complex of state and church buildings, rested on the belief in blood, all our present-day institutions rest on the belief in money, in real money. The former was superstition, but the latter is pure egotism. Reason destroyed the former; feeling will destroy the latter. The foundation of human society will some day be a better one, and all noble hearts of Europe

are agonizingly engaged in discovering this new and better basis.[26] (246-7)

Heine's critical vision, with its attention drawn in two directions at once, is now able to turn a sympathetic eye to the past, and to those Romantics who sought an escape from a crass present into a dream of the past:

> Perhaps it was dissatisfaction with the present belief in money and disgust at the egotism they saw sneering out everywhere that had first moved certain poets of the Romantic School in Germany with the best of intentions to flee from the present age to the past and to promote the restoration of medievalism. (247)

Romantic escapism is here observed as a critical gesture, an attack upon present meanness akin to Baudelaire's famous cry: "Anywhere out of the world."

Heine's method, which is to insist that no judge can be an advocate in his own cause, subjects the self-representations of the Romantic School to a sustained and vigorous critique. His justification for doing so rests upon the resolute character of his method, which systematically lays Heine himself and his immediate culture open to criticism. We shall observe this more particularly later; here I want to instance only the most dramatic example of Heine's procedure.

Toward the end of Book II of the essay Heine examines the work of Novalis and Hoffmann and seems to conclude in a rather mordant fashion.

> The great similarity between the two poets probably lies in the fact that their poetry was in reality a disease. It has been said in regard to this that the judgment of their writings is not the business of the critic but of the physician. The rosy light in the works of Novalis is not the color of health but of tuberculosis, and the fiery glow in Hoffmann's *Fantastic Tales* is not the flame of genius but of fever. (215)

But immediately Heine steps back as he recalls himself and his audience to the present and to those more paramount concerns which must underlie all acts of poetry and criticism if they are not to be merely precious, academic exercises.

But do we have a right to such remarks, we who are not all too blessed with health ourselves? Especially now, when literature looks like a huge hospital? Or is poetry perhaps a disease of mankind, as the pearl is really only the morbid substance from which the poor oyster beast is suffering?

Heine's sympathetic critique of Romanticism in Germany might well be—and, indeed, here will be—a model of critical procedure. The power of the essay lies in its double vision, which asks the critic to call into question those representations which a cultural subject offers as an explanation of itself. In fact, if we reflect upon the theories of Romanticism advanced by the critics we have already considered, we shall not fail to see the extent to which each has embraced one or more aspects of his subject's original attitudes and convictions. These acts of acceptance create the fault lines in the theories, and they begin to appear when a Lovejoyan argument-by-exception is instituted: thus Abrams' theory cannot accommodate certain phenomena epitomized by Byron.

The fact is—and Heine's essay shows itself fully alive to this matter—that important cultural phenomena subject themselves to criticism at all times. To the degree that a later critical assessment cannot emulate the initial self-criticism which significant cultural products call out or generate, to that degree the later criticism has been consumed by its own ideology. Heine's essay repeatedly illustrates this view, not least memorably when he denounces the period of German philosophy dominated by Hegel:

> After him [Schelling] our philosophers . . . sought reasons for justifying the *status quo*; they became vindicators of what exists . . . ; they became state philosophers, for they invented philosophical justifications for all the interests of the state in which they were employed. . . .
>
> Yes, just as once the Alexandrian philosophers summoned all their ingenuity to preserve, through allegorical interpretations, the declining religion of Jupiter from total downfall, so our German philosophers are attempting something similar for the religion of Christ. We care little about examining whether these philosophers have a disinterested aim, but when we see them allied with the

36

> party of priests whose material interests are connected
> with the preservation of Catholicism, we call them
> Jesuits. They should not think, however, that we are
> confusing them with the earlier Jesuits. They were great
> and powerful, full of wisdom and strength of will. Alas
> for the feeble dwarfs who fancy they would overcome
> the difficulties which were the ruin of even those black
> giants! Never has the human mind invented grander
> dialectics than those with which the ancient Jesuits tried
> to preserve Catholicism. (212-13)

Unlike those works of art which are its subject matter, literary criticism shares the danger which Heine here reveals about philosophy (and especially speculative and systematic philosophy). This is why the ideologies which appear through the mediation of art—the thematic self-representations of poetry—must not be uncritically embraced by later minds. To generate a polemic for Romantic poetry on its own ideological terms at this point in time is to vitiate criticism and to court mere intellectual sentiment.[27] The latter is the farce of Romanticism's original tragic nostalgia—an historical repetition which Byron once called "man's worst, his second fall."

Let me give two examples before moving to the next phase of this paper. In an important essay on Romanticism Morse Peckham argued that the movement was characterized by a profound crisis of culture, and that it met this crisis with a "psychological strategy . . . of cultural alienation and social isolation." Hegel's *Phenomenology*, Peckham asserts, "was at once the profoundest response to the crisis and the profoundest theory of it." From this Peckham argues that "all students of Romanticism . . . should read" this work "repeatedly," and he goes on to explain his reasons:

> No one responded so completely to the crisis; no one's
> response was so pure, so free of non-Romantic notions
> inconsistent with the Romantic anti-metaphysical meta-
> physic; no one made so thorough-going an attempt to
> comprehend what was happening. The *Phenomenology*
> was at once the profoundest response to the crisis and
> the profoundest theory of it.[28]

Peckham's view of Hegel (though not his attitude toward Hegel) is quite in agreement with Heine's as he expressed himself in

The Romantic School and *The History of Religion and Philosophy*. Heine departs from Peckham on the issue of criticism: for where Peckham, from his vantage in 1970, asks us to embrace Hegel's explanation of Romanticism, Heine urges that we study the explanation from the critical posture which history expects of us. From the vantage of Hegel's period we might want to say that the *Phenomenology* was the profoundest response to the crisis of Romanticism; but Hegel's response, as even Peckham insists, is a document so absorbed by its own subject that, from our critical vantage, we can only follow its procedures to our peril. Today no criticism of the Romantic Movement can seek to be "free of non-Romantic notions" if it means to be taken seriously as criticism.

Thus Mellor's critique of Abram's theory begins in strength but ends weakly. Its strength lies in its clear sense that Abrams has uncritically accepted a Wordsworthian-Coleridgean ideology of Romanticism. Its weakness emerges when we observe Mellor's decision not to subject that ideology to a critical analysis, but to accept and modify it. Mellor will reconcile those old enemies, Wordsworth and Byron, via an uncritical use of the concept of Romantic Irony. This impulse to seek reconciliations is, indeed, a central Romantic preoccupation, as we all know, and Mellor lends that impulse her uncritical support in her book. But all reconciliations are not the same, and one might well think, with Blake, that two classes of men such as Byron and Wordsworth "are always upon earth" and, further, that "whoever seeks to reconcile them seeks to destroy existence." Within the field of Romantic conflicts and crises which so many critics have emphasized,[29] the most fruitful sort of reconciliations to be made are often dialectical rather than synthetic. What Coleridge meant by "the One Life" seemed to Byron "a narrowness," a purely conceptual unity achieved at the expense of experience, where one knew that "the field is universal" rather than unified.[30]

The erosion of Mellor's critical position appears most clearly in her enthusiastic polemic for an intrinsic value within the concept of Romantic Irony, as well as in her allied refusal to take serious account of Kierkegaard's more somber thematic assessment of the concept. Heine's remarks on Romantic Irony are most instructive in this context, for they are able to move easily between the shifting poles of judgment and sympathy which criticism is always obliged to negotiate.

> We talk a good deal about this humorous irony, the
> Goethean school of art praises it as a special excellence
> of their master, and it now plays a large role in German
> literature. But it is only a sign of our lack of political
> freedom, and as Cervantes had to take refuge in
> humorous irony at the time of the Inquisition in order
> to intimate his ideas without leaving a weak spot
> exposed for the serfs of the Holy Office to seize upon, so
> Goethe also used to say in a tone of humorous irony
> what he, as minister of state and courtier, did not dare
> to say outright. Goethe never suppressed the truth;
> when he could not show it naked, he clothed it in
> humor and irony. Especially writers who languish
> under censorship and all kinds of restrictions on free-
> dom of thought and yet can never disavow their heart-
> felt opinion have to resort to the ironic and humorous
> manner. It is the only solution left for honesty, and in
> this disguise such honesty is revealed most movingly.
> (204)

Heine's method is profoundly critical largely because it is so systematically self-critical and exploratory. He views his subject
from a distance which permits him to analyze and judge his
materials, but at the same time that distance gives his subject
matter the power to qualify his critical judgments. Thus Heine's
sardonic comments on the German School's use of Romantic
Irony succeed to a moment of sympathetic understanding and
conclude in a typical gesture of reversal: high praise for Tieck's
translation of *Don Quixote* and for the method of Romantic
Irony in general. Most important to note is Heine's understanding that "it was precisely the Romantic School that provided us
with the best translation of a book in which its own folly is
exposed so delightfully." Implicit in this judgment is a truly profound grasp of the critical history which great works of art are
continually engaged with.

4

The Line of Coleridge and the Line of Hegel:

Romantic Repetition and

Romantic Reification

We should now be in a position to provide a more general
assessment of the chief lines of Romantic criticism and what
they mean. I will begin with Geoffrey Hartman's influential
essay on Romanticism in which he demonstrates his own line of
continuity with his subject and its history. In Hartman's view,
the desire "to maintain something of the interacting unity of self
and life, is a central concern of the Romantic poets." The
Romantic poet "seeks a return to 'Unity of Being'. Consciousness is only a middle term, the strait through which . . . the
artist plots to have everything pass through whole."[31] Hartman's
remarks seem to me exact translations of those issues in Romanticism which are fundamental precisely because they were
declared to be fundamental by the earliest Romantics themselves.

In those early documents we observe a repeated concern to
achieve various types of harmonies, systems, and reconciliations,
and to establish these unified configurations in conceptual terms.
We observe as well what Wordsworth called "the anxiety of
[this] hope," that is, the feeling that the condition of harmony
has to be *returned to,* that the idea of unity has to be recovered
or reborn. This obsession with restoring what was
perceived—mythologically, in every sense—as a lost sense of
total order was a function of an age marked by extreme cultural
upheaval throughout Europe. Historians of ideas commonly
argue that the age's political and social turmoil was matched by
an "epistemological crisis"; the coincidence of these disruptive

forces represented themselves, at the cultural level, in a variety of so-called "Romantic" forms.

Hartman's formulations are well known because they represent a contemporary academic consensus about Romantic literature. The strength of the position lies in the accuracy with which it reflects, or translates, the original materials. His is what Peckham would call a "pure" response to Romanticism, that is, one which is, despite its new terminology, "free of non-Romantic notions inconsistent with the Romantic . . . metaphysic."[32] Its weakness, which is a function of that strength, lies in the uncritical employment of Romanticism's self-representing concepts. To reach a more generous critical understanding of Romanticism, even on its own terms, requires that we be able to assess and judge those terms—which is to say that we be able to see our object of inquiry in terms other than its own.

Let me begin at the level of ideology rather than at the level of artistic production. Of course, a comprehensive theory of Romanticism would demand an analysis of *all* the key ideological concepts of Romanticism. For the present I shall confine myself to one of these—the ideal of Harmony or "Unity of Being"—as it appears in the work of Coleridge, and then as it is later reassessed through Hegel and Heine. This idea becomes a philosophical goal of most Romantic theorists, all of whom have been marked by that sign of Cain, a passion for systematic knowledge (and generally, as with Coleridge and the German post-Kantians, for speculative systematic knowledge).

Coleridge said that his philosophic endeavor was to "reduce all knowledge into harmony . . . to unify the insulated fragments of truth, and therewith to frame . . . the whole truth." To do this, Coleridge argued, demanded that the truths and investigative methods of "the understanding" be subordinated to the integrative Method, the Whole Truth, of "the reason." "The English public" had to be led to "comprehend the essential difference between the reason and the understanding—between a principle and a maxim—an eternal truth and a mere conclusion generalized from a great number of facts."[33]

Coleridge's analysis of the scientific method—both in the "real" and in the historical sciences—is acute. First, the "real" sciences:

> The use of a theory in the real sciences is to help the
> investigator to a complete view of all the hitherto
> discovered facts relating to the science in question; it is
> a collected view . . . of all he yet knows in *one*. Of
> course, whilst any pertinent facts remain unknown, no
> theory can be exactly true, because every new fact must
> necessarily, to a greater or less degree, displace the rela-
> tion of all the others. A theory, therefore, only helps
> investigation; it cannot invent or discover. . . . [T]o sup-
> pose that, in our present exceedingly imperfect acquain-
> tance with the facts, any theory in chemistry or geology
> is altogether accurate, is absurd:—it cannot be true.[34]

Coleride's attack upon the "historical mode" of investigation is
congruent with these views on scientific method.

> The historical mode is a very common one: in it the
> author professes to find out the truth by collecting the
> facts of the case, and tracing them downwards; but . . .
> suppose the question is as to the true essence and char-
> acter of the English constitution. First, where will you
> begin your collection of facts? where will you end it?
> What facts will you select? and how do you know that
> the class of facts which you select, are necessary terms
> in the premises, and that other classes of facts, which
> you neglect, are not necessary? And how do you distin-
> guish phenomena which proceed from disease or
> accident, from those which are the genuine fruits of the
> essence of the constitution? What can be more striking,
> in illustration of the utter inadequacy of this line of
> investigation for arriving at the real truth, than the polit-
> ical treatises and constitutional histories which we have
> in every library? A Whig proves his case convincingly to
> the reader who knows nothing beyond his author; then
> comes an old Tory (Carte, for instance), and ferrets up a
> hamperful of conflicting documents and notices, which
> proves *his* case *per contra*. A. takes this class of facts; B.
> takes that class: each proves something true, neither
> proves *the* truth, or anything like *the* truth; that is, the
> whole truth.[35]

According to Coleridge, the weakness in the historical method
lies in its empirical, non-theoretic procedures. For him, "theory"
is crucial to both scientific and cultural studies; but whereas in
the inquiries of "real science" theory must always remain

hypothetical, in cultural investigations theory is what guarantees the possession of "the whole truth."

> You must therefore, commence with the philosophic idea of the thing, the true nature of which you wish to find out and manifest. You must carry your rule ready made, if you wish to measure aright. If you ask me how I can know that this idea—my own invention—is the truth, by which the phenomena of history are to be explained, I answer, in the same way exactly that you know that your eyes were made to see with; and that is, because you *do* see with them. If I propose to you an idea or self-realizing theory of the constitution, which shall manifest itself as in existence from the earliest times to the present,—which shall comprehend within it *all* the facts which history has preserved, and shall give them a meaning as interchangeably causals or effects;—if I show you that such an event or reign was an obliquity to the right hand, and how produced, and such other event or reign a deviation to the left, and whence originating,—that the growth was stopped here, accelerated there,—that such a tendency is, and always has been, corroborative, and such other tendency destructive, of the main progress of the idea towards realization;—if this idea, not only like a kaleidoscope, shall reduce all the miscellaneous fragments into order, but shall also minister strength, and knowledge, and light to the true patriot and statesman for working out the bright thought, and bringing the glorious embryo to a perfect birth;—then, I think, I have a right to say that the idea which led to this is not only true, but the truth, the only truth.[36]

This is a powerful polemic, all the more powerful because it is a polemic. Its authority rests on its appeal to what *is*, to what exists, to what is seen and believed to go on before Coleridge's eyes and the eyes of those around him. But we have to recognize that the argument is both enabled and limited by its social and historical interests. Coleridge, for example, looks to the future as to a continuation of the past, a "natural" extension from what he sees and knows rather than a surprising break or change from what is familiar to him. This assumption is what makes his mind a "conservative" one.

The fundamental weakness of Coleridge's position is plain enough, I suppose. He assumes that historical facts (in contrast to the facts of "real science") can be once and for all interpreted if only the investigator is able to grasp "the philosophic idea" of the subject at hand. Facts of science shift in time as investigations proceed, but cultural facts are *fixed* in time, and ask of the investigator only that he grasp that central "idea" of them which balances and reconciles all their opposite and discordant qualities. What Coleridge neglects to consider, however, is the social and historical transformations which cultural studies are subject to. His philosophic, totalizing grasp of cultural history—indeed, Hegel's systematic presentation of such a speculation—is not a universal, transcendant truth but a limited and time-specific idea. It is, in brief, an ideology of knowledge.

Elsewhere Coleridge discusses such matters more fully, and in a purely aesthetic context, but Hegel's treatment is at once more comprehensive and more normative, at least for European Romanticism. His presentation is structured in terms of a dialectic between Symbolic and Classical Art.

> Art begins when the spiritual idea, being itself still indefinite and obscure and ill-comprehended, is made the content of artistic forms. As indefinite, it does not yet have that individuality which the artistic idea demands; its abstractness and one-sidedness thus render its shape defective and whimsical. The first form of art is therefore rather a mere search after plasticity than a capacity of true representation. The spiritual idea has not yet found its adequate form, but is still engaged in striving and struggling after it. This form we may, in general, call the *symbolic* form of art; in such form the abstract idea assumes a shape in natural sensuous matter which is foreign to it; with this foreign matter the artistic creation begins, from which, however, it seems unable to free itself.[37]

Symbolic Art, characterized by various kinds of "incongruity," exaggeration, and discord, is unable to reconcile "its endless quest, its inner struggle" to bring together "the spiritual idea and the sensuous form" (322). In Classical Art, however, "we find the free and adequate embodiment of the spiritual idea in the form most suitable to it, and with it meaning and expression are in perfect accord" (323).

Hegel discerns an inadequacy in this Classical reconciliation because the "spiritual idea" of Classical Art is not transcendent but anthropomorphic: "The form in which the idea, as spiritual and individual, clothes itself when revealed as a temporal phenomenon, is *the human form*" (323). Hegel's totalizing categories are obliged to cast a negative judgment on such an art because "Spirit is characterized as a particular form of mind, and not as simply absolute and eternal" (324). But since "the absolute and eternal Spirit must be able to reveal and express itself in a manner far more spiritual," the "defect of classical art" is revealed. Art's "transition to a third and higher form, to wit, the *romantic* form of art," is demanded by what Coleridge would call "the philosophic idea" of the subject itself (324).

For Hegel, Romantic Art is explicitly Christian and specifically Protestant in form. In this art the "content" is "the unity of the human and divine nature," but not a unity achieved in "the sensuous, immediate existence of the spiritual"; rather it is a unity of "self-conscious and internal contemplation":

> The new content, won by this unity, is not dependent upon sensuous representation; it is now exempt from such immediate existence. In this way, however, romantic art becomes art which transcends itself, carrying on this process of self-transcendence within its own artistic sphere and artistic form. (326-7)

This form of art passes beyond the classical and anthropomorphic type to find "reconciliation only within the inner recesses of the spirit. This *inner* world is the content of romantic art." In such an art "The inner life thus triumphs over the outer world . . . [and] sensuous appearance sinks into insignificance" (327).

This situation does not mean that Romantic Art abandons concrete forms of representation. All art, Hegel says, "needs an external mode of expression," including Romantic Art. In the latter, however, "the sensuous externality of form assumes again, as it did in symbolic art, an insignificant and transient character." Romantic Art therefore constitutes a Symbolic Art raised to a higher level. The incongruities of Symbolic Art—what Lovejoy called, in relation to Romanticism, the "diversities," "peculiarities," and the "plenitude" of its forms—find a spiritual idea adequate to their endless transformations, which can be finally given free reign and full play in a Romantic Art:

> The external side of things is surrendered to accident
> and committed to the excesses of the imagination,
> whose caprice now mirrors existence as it is, now
> chooses to distort the objects of the outer world into a
> bizarre and grotesque medley, for the external form no
> longer possesses a meaning and significance, as in classi-
> cal art, on its own account and for its own sake. Feeling
> is now everything . . . .
> Hence, the indifference, incongruity, and antagon-
> ism of spiritual idea and sensuous form, the characteris-
> tics of symbolic art, reappear in the romantic type, but
> with this essential difference. In the romantic realm, the
> spiritual idea, to whose defectiveness was due the defec-
> tive forms of symbolic art, now reveals itself in its per-
> fection within mind and feeling. It is by virtue of the
> higher perfection of the idea that it shuns any adequate
> union with an external form, since it can seek and
> attain its true reality and expression best within itself.
> (327-8)

Hegel's and Coleridge's aesthetic accounts share a number of important elements, not the least of which is the commitment to a systematic method of presentation which is dynamic and dialectical in form. One need only compare Hegel's elaborate presentation, which I have just outlined, with Coleridge's pithy remarks in the *Table Talk* of 12 September 1831.[38] Coleridge's statement incorporates an arresting synoptic account of the dialectical and dynamic system which underlies his approach to all cultural phenomena.

What is even more interesting, however, are the differences which appear between Hegel and Coleridge. Hegel's account of art, like all his projects in philosophy, comprises a full and care-fully worked out speculative presentation. As Peckham has sug-gested, his theory of Romanticism is a "pure" one in the sense that it takes account of Romantic Art on its own terms. But the completeness of Hegel's thought, its comprehensive philosophic articulation, contrasts sharply with those central accounts of Romanticism which its practitioners themselves produced. Coleridge, who aspired to the systematic condition of Hegel, is a *Romantic* theoretician of Romanticism precisely because his theorizing is produced in scattered and unintegrated forms—in aphorisms, fragments, and partial or unfinished presentations. Coleridge's centrality as Romantic ideologue lies in this broken quality of his massive acts of cultural definition. The compass of his prose works is very large, but it rests—it triumphs—in its fragmentation.[39]

Hegel's theory of Romantic Art is important, then, precisely because it is a non-Romantic theory of its subject. Its non-Romantic character—the finishedness of its ideological presentation—highlights by contrast a crucial aspect of Coleridge's theorizing, which searches (in vain) for a systematic reconciliation of its contradictions. What Hegel says of Romantic art is not *in fact* true—Romanticism is characterized not by its reconciliations, its artistic completeness, but by its *Sehnsucht*, its fragmentations: by its aspirations toward that condition of reconciliation which Hegel ascribes to it. Hegel's account preserves the ideological terms of its subject—it is a "pure" theory—but it does so only in a formal and priestly way. For all its emphasis on "Spirit" and "spirituality," Hegel's theory has reproduced an abstract and sentimental Romanticism, the letter and not the spirit of its subject. Far from being a Romantic account of Romantic art, the Hegelian synthesis is a form of self-representation: it describes the idea of Hegel's philosophy and not Romantic art, nor even the Romantic ideology of art.

A systematic or comprehensive Romantic accounting of Romanticism—of its works or its ideology—is an impossibility: indeed, it is a contradiction in terms. The earliest Romantic theories of Romanticism are always cast in polemical, incomplete, or exploratory forms. They are manifestos, *aperçus*, or "spontaneous" and self-generated searches. These characteristics of Romantic thought, in prose and verse alike, are a sign of its aspiration toward completeness: a completeness of idea, a completeness of culture, perfection of art. In short, "Unity of Being." But what distinguishes Romantic forms from any synthetic representation of those forms is that the former's aspirations (and dissatisfactions) are preserved at the most radical level. Dissatisfaction cannot produce a satisfactory account of itself, only—as with Coleridge—a perfect account.

Consequently, the phenomena of Romanticism descend to us in three sorts of representations. Coleridge and Hegel epitomize the two which have most preoccupied scholars and critics, especially in the twentieth century, and Heine stands as the original form of the third. Coleridge's theory of Romanticism is the archtypical Romantic theory—brilliant, argumentative, ceaseless, exploratory, incomplete, and not always very clear. Hegel's theory, speculative and total, represents the transformation of Romanticism into acculturated forms, into state ideology. Hegel sentimentalizes Romanticism by domesticating its essential tensions, conflicts, and patterns of internal contradiction. Wordsworth's fearful "anxiety of hope," those "blank misgivings" which go to make up what he called "something evermore about to be," become through Hegel a Happy Valley for the reader. Its names now are legion and they all please: creative process, Romantic energy, poetry of encounter, and so forth. The academy today, its scholars and teachers, tend to follow some variant form of the Hegelian synthesis, though certain figures—Harold Bloom in particular—manifestly pursue a Romantic approach to the subject of Romanticism and its works.

Romanticism can be approached along another line altogether, however, the one initiated by Heine in *The Romantic School*. This method entails neither a repetition of the subject's forms and ideologies (Romantic Criticism) nor a reification of such forms and their ideologies (Hegelian Criticism). The latter is an especially dangerous method since it represents the seizure of (past) artistic documents and the transformation of their initial human insights (which are therefore also critical insights, however unselfconscious) into present cultural slogans. Among those idols of our present caves we have already noted in passing the ideals of creative imagination, artistic autonomy, and poetic wholeness, as well as the hermeneutic models which continue to dominate academic criticism. The latter reconstitute literary works in the present through a process of thematization, that is, by reconciling past works with the dominant ideological constructs of the immediate culture.

By contrast, Heine's approach is analytic and critical; it assumes an antithetical but non-Romantic point of view toward its subject. The method draws past works of art into a present proximity in order that a dialectical encounter between subject and object can serve to criticize and illuminate both. The method does not involve a reconciliation of opposite and discordant materials but, rather, a struggle to maintain the two in an enlightening conflict. Secondary in its critical position, dialectical in its procedures, and historical in its orientation, this method may be usefully examined if we wish to understand the limits of the Hegelian and Coleridgean models, and perhaps to go beyond them.

5

A Critical Theory of Romanticism:

Heine on Uhland

(The Romantic School, Book III)

The outlines of Heine's method emerge most clearly—that is, in their most economical yet complete form—in his discussion of Ludwig Uhland's poetry in Book III of *The Romantic School*. The commentary begins with a slightly ironic apology.

> But I beg you to take into consideration the conditions under which I am writing, the time and place. Twenty years ago—I was a boy—yes, then, with what abounding enthusiasm I could have celebrated the excellent Uhland! Then I felt his excellence perhaps better than now; he was closer to me in thought and feelings. But since then so much has happened! What seemed to me so splendid, that chivalrous, Catholic world, those knights who cut and thrust at each other in aristocratic tournaments, those gentle squires and well-bred noble ladies, those Nordic heroes and Minnesingers, those monks and nuns, those ancestral vaults and awesome shudders, those pallid sentiments of renunciation to the accompaniment of bellringing, and the everlasting melancholy wailing—how bitterly it has been spoiled for me since then! (259)

The immediate cause of Heine's lament will be found in the section of the third book which he has just concluded. In it he had started to write an enthusiastic commentary on Uhland but, reflecting upon the present condition of the German theatre, Heine let himself be waylaid into a severe notice of the insipid works of Raupach and Madame Charlotte Birch-Pfeiffer. As Heine observes, "their success in the German theatre" represents the degraded state of "the contemporary world of the stage" in Germany (258).

The principal commentary on Uhland, then, resumes a discussion begun earlier, and the interruption has forced Heine to think of Uhland's poetry from a double vantage: on the one hand Heine recalls, in a mood of gentle irony, his early enthusiasm for Uhland's Romantic poetry when he read those works in Germany in 1813; on the other, he is aware that the passage of twenty years, and his own transportation to France, has forever altered his original sense of Uhland's work.

> I hold this same volume in my hands once more, but twenty years have passed since then, I have heard and seen much in the meantime, a very great deal, I no longer believe there are people without heads, and the old spectral show no longer has any effect on my feelings. The house in which I am sitting and reading is on the Boulevard Montmartre; here the wildest waves of the times break; here screech the loudest voices of the modern age; there is laughing, roaring, and beating of drums; the National Guard marches past in double-quick time; and everyone is speaking French.—Is this the place to read Uhland's poems? (261)

Heine's is the most fundamental question which can be asked about works of a past or an alien culture, especially if we receive those works through our own earlier experience of them. What relevance can they have for us now; indeed, what authority can our own previous experience of them be allowed to exert? One cannot repudiate the past, but neither can one feed upon the dead. How do we negotiate between the authority of what has changed and the authority of what remains? "Is this the place to read Uhland's poems?"

The answer to this question is "yes." Heine writes a lengthy and generous commentary on Uhland here, and he quotes in full—himself re-reads and forces us to read—two of Uhland's old Romantic poems: the one a Romantic literary ballad of the past ("Der Schäfer"), the other an anti-Napoleonic marching song ("Vorwärts!"). But of course he does not read Uhland now in the same way that he once did. Heine's discussion is marked throughout by a bemused tone which signals his consciousness of a radical difference between 1813 and 1833. Indeed, in 1813 he read Uhland in a fully Romantic mode, "with a voice somewhat raised to overcome the mysterious awe inspired in me by the ancient castle ruins" (260) among which he had sat down to pour over Uhland. But now it is 1833 and *non sum qualis eram*.

Yet for Heine it is this very difference which matters. An epochal division separates 1833 and 1813 and Heine asks us to observe that differential as it was registered through a peculiar experience of his own. As far as the reader is concerned—a person very much in Heine's polemical mind—those experiences are important because they bring into focus certain objective historical circumstances. Heine's personal history is offered to the reader as a paradigm for any reader of literary works. Heine shares with his original (1833) audience the context and general point of view of 1833; but ultimately 1833 will become an historical sign to the later reader that when works are read anew, they must be read within the structure of an historical dialectic precisely like Heine's.

In Heine's view, Uhland is an important poet whose works, though now "dated," acquire a new force when considered in relation to present needs and conditions. In the first place, the debased contemporary German theatre is brought to judgment by the past when Heine compares the dramas of Raupach and Birch-Pfeiffer with Uhland's *Duke Ernst of Swabia.* Worthy literary works of the past always possess this function, that they set a measure by which present work can be—must be—assessed. Among those who have ears to hear, the noble living are born from the noble dead.

In the second place, Heine argues that Uhland's works are progressive and critical even in their afterlife of 1833. The two poems he quotes are shrewdly chosen for this argument. "Der Schäfer" is for him a ballad which foretells the passing of its own dream, and hence which teaches an early and crucial lesson in criticism and self-consciousness. It narrates the story of the love of a shepherd for a maiden in a tower, and of her reciprocal longing for him. An emblem of Romantic *Sehnsucht*, their mutual desire ends without fulfillment, as it does in Keats's more famous English ballad on the same topic.

> The winter went, back came the spring,
> And flowers bloomed around.
> The shepherd passed the castle's wing,
> His love no more he found.
>
> The shepherd cried, an anguished moan,
> "Hail, lovely princess fair and fine!"
> Down came a muffled, ghostly tone,
> "Farewell, O shepherd mine!"

When Heine comes to read this ballad from the vantage of 1833 he reads not "the poem itself" but the experienced poem, the work as it exists in social space (the only form in which it can exist). Contemporary formalist critics might say that Heine reads his own reading of the ballad, but this formulation would not be correct enough, though superficially it appears to be the case.

Sitting amid the ruins of the old castle and reciting this poem, I sometimes heard the nymphs in the Rhine, which flows by there, imitating my words, and from the waters came a sighing and a moaning with a comical pathos:

> Down came a muffled, ghostly tone,
> "Farewell, O shepherd mine!"

But I ignored the chaffing of the nymphs, even when they giggled ironically at the most beautiful passages in Uhland's poems. (260)

Heine's brilliant commentary reminds us of two important facts about all poetic interpretations. First, by insisting upon the emblematic quality of the ballad Heine shows that when he read it in 1813 his reading was not personal but typical: it was a Romantic reading fully in sympathy with the ballad's own thematized narrative. Second, Heine's commentary shows that Uhland's ballad—once again, not the poem itself—passes an ironical judgment upon this Romantic reading. In 1813 Heine was himself vaguely aware of this irony but he chose to ignore it and to follow the impulse of his Romantic enthusiasm. With the passage of twenty years, however, he sees very clearly what he was only able to intuit in a vague way in 1813.

"We love and honor [Uhland] now perhaps all the more," Heine says, "because we are about to part from him forever." (268) By this Heine does not mean to say that Uhland's poetry will henceforth be relegated to the antiquarian and the philologist; on the contrary, these poems retain their power just because they are themselves so aware of their historical particularity—are "so impregnated with the spirit of their time"—that they speak to the present of a perpetual future.

> And we can readily understand that our excellent Uhland's ballads and romances found the greatest favor not simply among the patriots of 1813, among upright youths and lovely maidens, but also among many persons endowed with greater powers and among many modern thinkers. (264)

Uhland can speak to the future, Heine argues, because that is what he was committed to. His poetry never rests satisfied with itself and hence always transmits a perpetual message to the future of the need for a committment to progressive change. Uhland's poetry is part of—will always be part of—what Heine calls the "War of Liberation."

> I have added the year 1813 to the word "patriots" in order to distinguish them from present-day patriots, who no longer live off the memories of the so-called War of Liberation. Those older patriots must derive the sweetest pleasure from Uhland's muse, since most of his poems are completely impregnated with the spirit of their time, a time when they themselves were reveling in youthful emotions and proud hopes. They passed on the preference for Uhland's poems to their disciples. (264)

Heine's proof of this position is twofold. First, he points out that Uhland forsook his poetry in the latter part of his career in order to become "an ardent representative of the rights of the people in the Württemberg Diet" and "a bold speaker for civic equality and freedom of thought." Uhland's life and his poetry are intimately connected; the life seems to fulfill the poetry just as the poetry justified the life (and vice versa):

> precisely because his intentions toward the modern age
> were so honorable, he could no longer keep on singing
> the old song about ancient times with his old
> enthusiasm. (262)

Uhland's career in politics underscores the self-critical and progressive character of his poetry. More significantly, that career
raises Uhland's work out of its mere academic and literary history and places it in an essential relation to epochal history. This
placement, which is central to Heine's aesthetic argument, fully
reveals the social and historical nexus which all literary works
are involved with, even the dreamiest works of a Romantic poet
like Uhland.

Thus, although Heine's remarks on Uhland's Romantic ballad already demonstrated poetry's self-critical powers, his commentary on Uhland's marching song is even more telling since it
definitely places those powers within an historical setting which
is calling out for human commitments. This song, which cele-
brates the "War of Liberation" as it was being waged in the 1813
struggles against Napoleon, urges in 1833 a new message of progress and self-criticism.

The career of Adelbert von Chamisso is now introduced to
crown Heine's argument. Unlike Uhland, Chamisso never
entered the field of politics, but the significance of Chamisso's
work remains clear because Uhland stands as its explanatory
paradigm. This is why Heine says that he must "still praise some
members of the Romantic School" (266).

> Although a contemporary of the Romantic School, in
> whose activities he took part, yet this man's heart has in
> recent times been so wonderfully rejuvenated that he
> modulated to completely different keys, had an
> influence as one of the most original and most impor-
> tant modern poets, and belongs far more to *young Ger-
> many* than to *old Germany*. (267)

Indeed, they speak more to the present—any and every
present—precisely because, in the past, they had so fully embo-
died the commitments of their epoch. As Romantics they were
absorbed in their dreams of the old Germany, but it was just
those dreams, of a light that never was on sea or land, which
served to deliver them over to the realities of the present and its

new commitments.

Chamisso and Uhland transcended their original historical circumstances by writing poetry which took as its central subjects (a) the necessity of historical self-criticism, and (b) the obligation to speak with a voice whose full contemporaneity is only achieved through a vision of the future, a sense of the imperatives which drive what is present toward what must come. Uhland's present, in 1813, is first adequately defined, in 1833, in Heine's commentary.

> Oh, not from a frivolous whim, but obeying the law of necessity, Germany is stirring.—Pious, peaceful Germany!—It casts a melancholy glance at the past it leaves behind, once more it bends tenderly over the ancient era which gazes at us, so deathly pale, from Uhland's poems, and it bids farewell with a kiss. And another kiss, even a tear, for all I care! But let us tarry no longer in idle compassion.—
>
> > Forward, forward, one and all!
> > France now sounds the valiant call:
> > Forward! (268)

That wonderful irony—"even a tear, for all I care" ("meinetwegen sogar eine Thräne!")[40]—defines the non-Romantic character of Heine's sympathy with his Romantic subject. It is, besides, perfectly true to Heine, since it recalls those giggling nymphs of the Rhine which Heine, in 1813, had heard whispering between the lines of Uhland's ballad, but whose words he could not then fully understand.

Is this the place to read Uhland's poem then? Heine's answer is not merely "yes," it is stronger still. "This" is always the place to read important works of the past because "this" is the place where the future always has its relation to the past defined. Uhland's poems belong to 1833 only because they were so fully engaged with their own age and circumstances: "the spirit of [1813 is] splendidly preserved in Mr. Uhland's poems, and not simply the political, but also the moral and esthetic spirit" (265). Uhland's Romanticism, with its commitments to the images of a Catholic and medieval past, gives to his poems, as initially produced, their special historical significance. Indeed, Uhland's Romanticism causes his poetry to be completely inbued with that critical self-consciousness which becomes clarified in its historical self-consciousness. This characteristic of Uhland's poetical work forces a reciprocating historical self-consciousness upon Heine, and causes his commentary to organize itself around a dialectical discourse between people and events of 1813 and those later people and events of 1833. Heine means that dialectic to serve as a model for all later critics and readers.

Needless to say, such a critical dialectic is only possible if the historical uniqueness of subject and object is carefully preserved. To do this means that the critic must be as much "subject to" the judgment of his critical "object" as that object is subjected to his criticism. Subject and object must interchange their relations with each other, as we observed in Heine's commentary on Uhland. To achieve this result requires the most accurate (historical) definition of the terms of the critical discourse: the subject, the object, and the audience. Criticism is built upon a clear view of relevant differentials. Historical criticism is the completed form of criticism because it establishes the ground on which such differentials can be adequately and fully articulated.

PART II

Romantic Ideas,
Romantic Poems,
Romantic Ideologies

6

The Mental Theatre of Romantic Poems

Heine is an interesting, perhaps a crucial figure in the critical history of Romanticism because he developed a method which could resume his subject without suffering at the same time either the fire of repetition or the ice of reification. Though the broad cultural import of this freedom is important, my immediate concern is to explore its significance in that narrowest and most cloistered of spheres: in the critical work produced by the literary academy. In this world Heine has had little direct influence, partly because he is such a renegade figure, and partly because his is an artist's criticism, not a scholar's. But Heine is important for academic criticism because he was the first to attempt a comprehensive critical analysis of Romanticism along historical and ideological lines. Like the *De L'Allemagne* of Mme de Staël before him, which was the antithetical model for Heine's *Die romantische Schule*, Heine dealt with Romanticism as a cultural phenomenon, and he saw that the significance of its artistic works lay precisely in their power to exert a continuous cultural influence. Romantic poems were important because of the fact that, and the way that, they acted as the vehicles of ideology. Heine separated himself from Mme de Staël because he approached his subject not as a propagandist but as a critic.

Heine's work helps us to understand the intimate relation which subsists between poetical works and ideological structures, which is the topic I now wish to explore in greater depth. Reading him we see why we cannot follow the lead of L. J. Swingle, who recently urged the academy to abandon the traditional scholar's obsession with an "adequate theory of Romanticism."[1] The struggles epitomized in the clash between Lovejoy and Wellek are beside the point since, in Swingle's view, they cannot help us to elucidate the actual *works* of the poets. Romantic ideas and "doctrines" are one thing, but Romantic poems are quite another.

> Romanticism has to do with a fundamental state of
> mind, with patterns of ontological and normative

59

commitments. One can think of it as the state of mind out of which Romantic poetry is generated, or as the state of mind toward which Romantic poetry moves, or perhaps even as both. But Romantic poetry itself, while related in complex ways to this state of mind, is not identical with it. To come to terms with Romantic poetry, we have to deal with activities rather than with "states." Our concern is with immediate means and ends, with movements the poet attempts to accomplish, and ways in which he attempts to manipulate the reader. If things are working well, the poetry is like a drama which the reader becomes caught up in. To get into the poetry successfully, what is needed is not so much a theory of Romanticism but a theory of Romantic poetry, a model of the drama the poetry creates, something which explores the manipulations the poet exercises upon us as we read his poetry. (974)

Swingle's essay has gained some currency[2] and I will be considering it here from several angles. First, I agree with his general position, that our concern as scholars and critics must ultimately lie with the individual work rather than with our procedures for dealing with those works. And I also find persuasive a number of his remarks about the skeptical devices of Romantic poems. Finally, however, the essay interests me for a weakness which appears symptomatic of so much recent scholarship and criticism, both the best and worst of it: the inability to analyze, to draw out and define, the distinctive features of those cultural phenomena knows as poems when problems of periodization intervene.

Swingle's aim is to isolate the special character of Romantic poems so that we may read them more accurately. His argument proper begins with an attempt to distinguish Romantic poetry as non-doctrinal, as a poetry of exploration, of search and questioning: "The main product of Romantic poetry is the question, and its main effect on a reader is disturbance" (976). In this, Romantic poetry is said to differ from other, and particularly earlier, sorts of poetry.

Like any poetry, Romantic poetry is full of doctrinal elements. But it is important to think about what part these elements play in the poems. A poem can be designed to communicate doctrine, explain its meaning or implications, convince the reader of the truth or use-fulness of a given doctrine—in which cases doctrine plays the leading role in the poem: it is what the poem is about. (974-5)

Pope, but especially Sidney, provide Swingle with two exam-ples of what he means by "doctrinal" poetry. In the end both serve to establish the following position:

Rather than raising questions in order to move toward a presentation of doctrine, Romantic poetry tends to do quite the opposite: it employs doctrine in order to gen-erate an atmosphere of the open question. (975)

This pointed and economical statement is later supplemented with Swingle's more elaborated view—dare one say doctrine?—of the typical Romantic poem:

Such poetry involves a restructuring of traditional con-ceptions about what poetry is supposed to offer a reader. (Thus we often find the Romantic poet considering his work as "experiment.") True to tradition, this poetry seeks to offer a combination of instruction and delight. But the meaning of these terms has changed. Teaching does not mean offering answers to the reader's ques-tions, playing Sherlock Holmes to the reader's Watson. And the delight offered is not the satisfaction that accompanies a resolution of tension. Quite the opposite: Romantic poetry teaches by questioning the reader's answers. It guides by producing rather than relieving tension. It does not present the result of a quest, but instead forces the reader to experience the act of quest-ing himself. And the delight produced is that of a quest in process: the intellectual excitement of exposing false certainties, illuminating unconsidered complexities and new possibilities; the very opening out of intellectual horizons that accompanies the experience of grappling with uncertainties. (976)

Swingle's position is not far removed from the "poetry of encounter" we saw earlier in Barth's analysis of Romanticism, and the sorts of objections that were raised at that time remain pertinent here.[3] Reading this passage from Swingle one inevitably recalls *Surprised by Sin* and the entire project of so-called Reader-response criticism.

Nevertheless, what Swingle says obviously has a relevance to the strategy of Romantic poems. Problems appear because the terms of distinction—between Romantic (non-doctrinal) verse on the one hand, and "doctrinal" poetry on the other—seem to me particularly gross. The idea that "doctrine plays the leading role" in Pope's or Sidney's work, whereas in Wordsworth's or Byron's it will "play a supporting role," is a most misleading one to advance, particularly in an age and culture like our own where "doctrinal" poetry is virtually a synonym for the unpoetical. Such commonplace biases are in fact assumed by Swingle's argument, which seeks, among other things, to persuade us of the importance of Romantic poetry. But one ought not to do this at such a cost as Swingle has paid, for the transaction has subtly debased the work of Pope and Sidney, among others.

Besides, non-Romantic poetry is hardly well characterized when it is said to produce "the satisfaction that comes from the resolution of tension." Romantic poetry, on the other hand, "guides by producing rather than relieving tension." But surely the resolution of tension is a strange rubric under which to marshall the older literary works which we most value. One is flooded with contrary instances that range from *Beowulf* through the great Middle English ballads and lyrics to *Lear* and the entire compass of Renaissance and eighteenth-century works. One might just as profitably read the *Essay on Man* in terms of the *Dunciad* or *Gulliver* as through the treatises of Shaftesbury and Archbishop King.[4] Nor am I speaking here of *exceptions* to Swingle's formulation; on the contrary, the formulation will not do as a measure for distinguishing Romantic from "doctrinal" poetry. In fact, when Swingle says that Romantic poetry "forces the reader to experience the act of questing itself" he is not describing a special feature of *Romantic* poetry; he is setting forth one of our age's most basic value measures for any and all poetry. We will recognize this to be the case when we reflect how often we have heard the same thing said of every sort of poem ranging from the earliest to the most contemporary.

But if Swingle's formulation distorts our view of poetry in general, it obscures as well the importance of doctrine or ideology in Romantic verse. Do we really wish to say that doctrine plays a supporting role in Shelley's satiric thrusts against the

Holy Alliance, the English government, or the various ideologues of those institutions? Are Byron's *Don Juan* or *Vision of Judgment* non-doctrinal? Because the doctrines in these works are politically advanced we generally find it easy to sympathize with them, thence to translate them into our own (invisible) doctrines, and ultimately to forget—to our cost, in my view—that these are aggressively doctrinal works, and that they are important for that very reason.

Swingle either does not see these doctrinal aspects of Romantic poems, or he relegates them to supporting roles. The first result occurs because much Romantic verse—not Byron's of course—seeks to disguise its doctrinal material. More on this crucial matter in a moment.[5] The second result, however, is part of a conscious critical strategy. Swingle relegates Romantic doctrine to a supporting role because he has—correctly, I believe—responded to a special feature of Romantic style which is quite different from the style of earlier verse. He refers to it in various ways; traditionally it has been called "sincerity" or Romantic "spontaneity." These now old-fashioned terms point to a set of stylistic conventions developed by the Romantics to give the illusion of "spontaneous overflow" to their verse. This illusion creates in its turn the effect of "process" which Swingle speaks about. In Romantic poems we will characteristically follow the play or development of ideas, the movement of consciousness in its search for what it does not know that it knows.

This stylistic feature of many Romantic poems persuades Swingle that such poetry employs ideology only to call it into question. So he argues that "the Romantic poets [do not] seek predominantly to tell us things, that they [do not] write . . . a poetry of doctrine, offering the 'Isms' of Romanticism for reader consumption" (974). In this respect they are said to contrast with "doctrinal" poems of earlier periods, and Swingle uses Sidney's fine sonnet "Leave me O love" to illustrate his point. I shall have to examine Swingle's argument here in some detail since it demonstrates certain assumptions which seem to me quite wrong.

After quoting the first four lines of the sonnet Swingle says that

Sidney's thinking here is based upon certain assumptions about the mind's activity in the presence of mutable and eternal things—the assumption, for example, that the relationship between the human mind and a mutable love is a "pleasure" experience. (979)

By contrast, Romantic poems offer "us tests for such assumptions," and he quotes the final four lines of Wordsworth's "A slumber did my spirit seal" to demonstrate the difference:

> We ourselves are drawn into the experience of earthly love's mutability; our minds' reaction tests the validity of an order constructed upon the doctrine, "Leave me O Love." Is our reaction one of "fading pleasure"? If not, something is amiss at the basis of Sidney's conception. . . .Is the human mind able to "grow rich" in what "never taketh rust"? Can the mind in fact establish a relationship with something eternal? If not, if eternal objects in Keats's phrase only "tease us out of thought," then something is wrong with a conception of order based upon the assumption that the mind flourishes in the presence of eternity. (979)

Two fundamental problems haunt this passage. The first involves the travesty of Sidney's poem, which in this presentation becomes a curiosity of historical wrong-headedness. This is a reading which has removed the sonnet from our hands by telling us, not only that it is a simple piece of didacticism, but that its doctrine is naive and its "conception of order" wrong. This view patently violates our sense of the greatness and subtlety of the sonnet.

Let me quote Sidney's poem here in full and supply it with a brief alternative commentary.[6]

> Leave me O Love, which reachest but to dust,
> And thou my mind aspire to higher things:
> Grow rich in that which never taketh rust:
> What ever fades, but fading pleasure brings.
>
> Draw in thy beames, and humble all thy might,
> To that sweet yoke, where lasting freedomes be:
> Which breakes the clowdes and opens forth the light,
> That doth both shine and give us sight to see.
>
> O take fast hold, let that light be thy guide,
> In this small course which birth drawes out to death,

And thinke how evill becommeth him to slide,
Who seeketh heav'n, and comes of heav'nly breath.
Then farewell world, thy uttermost I see,
Eternall Love maintaine thy life in me.

First, on the matter of conventions. If "to pose a question" is a common device in Romantic poetry, particularly at moments of ideological importance, Renaissance poems frequently resort to petition, prayer, or exhortation at similar junctures. Sidney's sonnet illustrates this tendency as it moves through a variety of exhortations to conclude in a frank prayer to "Eternal Love." The whole structure of the poem's syntax demonstrates a person who is speaking out of a condition of profound contradictions. Swingle says that the poem is built on "the assumption . . . that the relationship between the human mind and a mutable love is a 'pleasure' experience," which is true only in the sense that the poem is also built on another, contradictory assumption: that the relationship between the human mind—the seat of the intellective faculties—and mortal love is one of frustration and dissatisfaction.

What the sonnet assumes is a traditional mind-body dualism, and it constructs its poetic appeal by dramatizing what happens when "my mind" has allowed the body's eyes to tempt it from its proper objects (lines 5-8). The poem presents a tension between the body and the mind, and it locates the area of greatest struggle in the eyes—the least sensual of the body's faculties (according to tradition) and therefore the most intellectually seductive. The poem represents the mind's self-exhortation to "see" that the source of its danger lies in *not seeing* the crucial difference between erotic and intellectual vision, between the "light" in the mind and the beam in the eye. The poem, in short, treats a familiar human problem in a most distinctive (and distinguished) way. D. H. Lawrence altered the emphasis and referred to it as "sex in the *head*" (my italics). In Sidney we would call it rather "*sex* in the head."

This sonnet, then, does not simply begin with certain doctrinal assumptions; it begins in the midst of an emotional drama which it then proceeds to elaborate and define. What is moving about the poem, even now, is the clarity with which it has presented a complex moment of intense emotional struggle. What is important for criticism, however, is to see the place which doctrine and ideology occupy in the sonnet. The poem's trans-historical character does not reside in its ideas or themes; on the contrary, the sonnet continues to speak to us by virtue of its emotional syntax. Certain of the poem's ideas seem dated or even, perhaps, wrong; the human drama it presents is complete and true, however, and must surely seem as fresh today as it was for Sidney at the end of the sixteenth century.

But although we need to recognize this emotional truth in the poem, and to see as well that the place of verse is to represent the human face that is part of every truth (and every error), equally important to understand is the place of ideology and doctrine in transmitting such material. Ideology—what literary criticism traditionally sees as the thematic and doctrinal aspects of verse—gives to poetry its local habitation and a name. Without such dated (and datable) matters poems would have nothing by which to define and embody their trans-historical qualities. The locus of what is unique in a poem, so far as criticism is concerned, is to be found and studied in its ideological structure, that is, in all those elements of the work which seem most historically particular and least transcendent. Part of the power of Sidney's sonnet depends upon our recognizing the dated character of its beliefs and ideas; its speaker seems all the more our contemporary because we recognize how far he is removed from us in the set of his mind. Recognizing this, we can, to a degree, observe as well our own ways of thinking and feeling from an alien point of view. That alienated vantage, which is poetry's critical gift to every future age, permits us a brief objective glimpse at our world and our selves.

Understanding this should help us to see one of the fundamental ideological structures of Romantic poems. Swingle is correct, I believe, when he says that Romantic poetry often puts received and traditional ideas and doctrines "to the test." He wants us to believe that in this respect Romantic poems do not offer any ideology for reader consumption. But his conclusion does not follow. On the contrary, one basic doctrine which Romantic poems continually present for reader consumption is that they are innocent of moral or doctrinal commitments. The idea that "art is not among the ideologies" or—in its conservative formulation—that art speaks universal truths,[7] has a basis in traditional theory where concepts like "Natural Law" and "the Soul" were commonplace. Under such conditions poetry could maintain its polemical and doctrinal functions because (a) the doctrines it spelled out were taken to be "naturally" or "universally" true, or (b) the polemics it engaged in, as we see throughout the controversial poetry of the seventeenth century, involved conflicting universalistic interpretations of transient historical phenomena.

In the Romantic Period, however, the ground universals of a Natural Law philosophy had been undermined, largely through the development of historical studies and the emergence of a modern historical sense. No longer did human nature seem always and everywhere the same, and the celebrated "epistemological crisis" was the chief register of this new ideological fact. In Cantos I-II of *Childe Harold's Pilgrimage* Byron expressed both his cynicism over the vagueries of modern national character and his wonder at the diverse and shifting behavior of different peoples. His locus of observation, initially, was the Peninsular War, but Wordsworth—studying the cultural drama being played out in Revolutionary France—observed an analogous situation. During the latter events Wordsworth believed for a time that "human nature" was "being born again." A new world seemed about to replace the conflicted and historically fractured cultures which were coming to pieces in Europe in the 1790s. Instead Wordsworth (like Blake) discovered a revolution which seemed to repeat all the ancient evils.

The doctrinal structures which writers like Blake, Wordsworth, and Coleridge developed to meet these crises are well known and need not be rehearsed again. What I want to note is the emergence of the concepts of Romantic Nature and Imagination as touchstones of stability and order. The literature of the period is replete with examples demonstrating what Byron shows in the following passage from Canto III of *Childe Harold*, where he is reacting to his own extended meditation upon the ruinous state of Napoleonic Europe.[8]

> Away with these! true wisdom's world will be
> Within its own creation, or in thine
> Maternal Nature! for who teems like thee. (st. 46)

In moments of crisis the Romantic will turn to Nature or the creative Imagination as his places of last resort. Amidst the tottering structures of early nineteenth-century Europe, poetry asserted the integrity of the biosphere and the inner, spiritual self, both of which were believed to transcend the age's troubling doctrinal conflicts and ideological shifts.

No poem illustrates these matters better, even in its miniature compass, than "A slumber did my spirit seal,"[9] which Swingle offers as a non-doctrinal Romantic work.

> A slumber did my spirit seal;
>   I had no human fears:
> She seemed a thing that could not feel
>   The touch of earthly years.
>
> No motion has she now, no force;
>   She neither hears nor sees;
> Rolled round in earth's diurnal course,
>   With rocks, and stones, and trees.

The suggestive force of the lines depends in large part upon the witty play with words like "earthly" and "earth's." In stanza one "earthly" is associated with "human fears," with culture, consciousness, and the "earth" upon which men do their getting and spending. In stanza two, "earth's" refers to a very different place, one which is marked not by human fears but by the most ancient and dependable regularities, which are here associated with "rocks, and stones, and trees." The poem offers a pathetic message for an experience of the loss of someone beloved, a comfort which yet troubles our own inevitable "human fears," a solace which cannot—which would not—remove the sense of pity and loss. These are a set of human thoughts which lie too deep for tears.

What is most important for us to see, however, is that the poem would lose all its force and character did it not operate at an ideological level. Unlike the Sidney poem, where the conflict involves intellectual and cultural problems that are directly related to action and behavior, Wordsworth's poem is altogether more nuanced, suggestive, and interiorized. The death of a loved one has focused the speaker's lack of awareness not merely of the *fact* that this loved one might die, but of his own general thoughtlessness about the ultimate *significance* of such an event. Wordsworth's poem raises the experience of personal loss to such a level of abstraction that we too are forced to consider it in the most conceptual and apocalyptic terms. This is a death which asks the poet to formulate both the problem of the death and the solution to the problem in ultimate terms.

So, in the second stanza Wordsworth manipulates the initial "problem" of unconsciousness into an avenue of resolution. The ancient, dumb geosphere is instinct with (God's) spiritual life and order. It is an obscure but certain realm of secret, meaningful signs, and to decipher them is to be possessed of the ground of all contingent truths. It is the visionary's task and privilege to decipher these signs—in particular, the visionary poet's task. When Romantic poems deal with Nature and Imagination, then, they are invoking a specific network of doctrinal material. Ecological Nature is the locus of what is stable and orderly, and it is related to Imagination as a set of vital hieroglyphs is related to an interpretive key.

Out of these assumptions emerges that familiar argument of Romantic and Romantic-influenced works: that poetry, and art in general, has no essential relation to partisan, didactic, or doctrinal matters. Poetry transcends these things. The field of history, politics, and social relations is everywhere marked in the Romantic Period by complex divisions and conflicts previously unprecedented in Europe. Romantic poetry develops an argument that such dislocations can only be resolved beyond the realm of immediate experience, at the level of the mind's idea or the heart's desire. The Romantic position—it is an historically limited and determinate one—is that the poet operates at such levels of reality, and hence that poetry by its nature can transcend the conflicts and transiences of this time and that place.

This conviction leads Shelley to his famous declaration:

Poetry is indeed something divine. It is at once the centre and circumference of knowledge; it is that which comprehends all science, and that to which all science must be referred. It is at the same time the root and blossom of all other systems of thought; it is that from which all spring, and that which adorns all. . . . What were Virtue, Love, Patriotism, Friendship —what were the scenery of this beautiful Universe which we inhabit; what were our consolations on this side of the grave, and what were our aspirations beyond it, if Poetry did not ascend to bring light and fire from those eternal regions where the owl-winged faculty of calculation dare not ever soar?[10]

It equally lies behind Wordsworth's distinction, set forth in the "Preface" to *Lyrical Ballads*, between the truths of poetry and the knowledge of science. Coleridge's entire Kantian-based theory of poetry, as is well known, depends upon analogous notions of the autonomy of the poetic event (*not* the poetic object, which is a post-Romantic conception). For Coleridge, the poetic experience involved an encounter with "the One Life," with the essential and non-contingent "Ideas" of human nature. The polemic of Romantic poetry, therefore, is that it will not be polemical; its doctrine, that it is non-doctrinal; and its ideology, that it transcends ideology.

In Blake's poetry this message is conveyed via what Swingle and others have recognized as his work's dialectical procedures. But Blake's critical devices are not innocent of ideology. When his poems put traditional ideas to critical tests of various sorts, they do so in the conviction that the poetic vision reveals fundamental truth in a way which sets the poet apart from other men. As a result, the testing critique which Romantic poems direct toward received ideas is always allied to a polemic on behalf of the special privilege of poetry and art. The Romantic attitude ascribes to poetry a special insight and power over the truth. The historically determined character of this idea becomes quite clear if we simply compare Homer's attitude toward the poet with Wordsworth's or Coleridge's. Changed circumstances—we will take these matters up below—pushed the later Romantics, in particular Byron and Shelley, into a more seriously problematic relation to the Romantic ideas of the poet-as-*vates* and the special privileges of art. In them the so-called Romantic Conflict went much deeper than anything experienced by the earlier Romantics, and this later problematic eventually contributed to the breakup of Romanticism as a coherent movement.

I have spent a great deal of time here discussing the ideas and concepts and attitudes of Romantic writers. Such a rehearsal of what are familiar intellectual abstractions might well strike the reader as tedious. I have tried to return to this field of intellectual history not in order to recuperate or reinforce such concepts, but to lay them under a revisionary critique. Contrary to what Swingle suggests, literary criticism must take account of these ideological matters—these ever-present "Isms" of Romanticism—precisely because Romantic works engage with the world, seek to engage with the world, at the level of ideology. The poetic response to the age's severe political and social dislocations was to reach for solutions in the realm of ideas. The maneuver follows upon a congruent Romantic procedure, which is to define human problems in ideal and spiritual terms. To characterize the Romantic Period as one marked by an "epistemological crisis" is to follow Romanticism's own definition of its historical problems.

Of course, a critic must grant to Romantic works their special historical character. A history of ideas approach to Romantic Poetry and the Romantic Period is traditional (and necessary) for this very reason: it represents the originary terms in which Romantic works sought to cast their historical relations. Such an approach will only recapitulate the Romantic or Hegelian analysis, however, if it does not establish a critical and historical perspective upon the "Isms" of Romanticism.

Swingle attempts to gain this distance by denying that the ideologies of Romantic works have any crucial relevance to the analysis of the poetry. But this approach has merely agreed to de-historicize Romantic Poetry by refusing to accept its special, self-determined limits. Swingle's account of Romantic works turns them into a standard of poetic excellence that is based upon our current, late-Romantic ideas about what poetry is and ought to do. But neither poetry nor literary criticism operate in trans-historical realms; both are cultural phenomena which take part in the special, historically determinate characteristics of their time and place. The idea that poetry deals with universal and transcendent human themes and subjects is a culturally specific one, and it assumes different forms of expression in different epochs, depending upon the different historical circumstances that prevail. The Romantic form of that idea is one of its many guises, but from our cultural position it is a form of thought which must assume a peculiar and insistent importance; for our own assent to the idea is characteristically made only when we have first passed through those Romantic forms of thought.

7

Romantic and Non-Romantic Works:

Comparisons and Contrasts

Before turning to investigate some specific Romantic poems, let me set forth a few brief comparisons between non-Romantic and Romantic works. This move seems necessary before proceeding any further, since the generalizations I have been advancing are liable to serious misinterpretation. It would, of course, be simple enough to set certain types of poems against typical Romantic works and thereby urge the distinctiveness of the Romantic: we could turn to Crabbe in the Romantic Period; or to Pope, Chaucer, or any number of Medieval secular lyrics; or (in post-Romantic contexts) to Clough, Pound, Marianne Moore, or many others. But if such examples would set Romantic poetry apart, they would not argue the case of my representation of Romantic works.

To argue the latter position requires that we look at some poems which deal in a non-Romantic way with "universal and transcendent human themes and subjects," which seek to "define human problems in ideal and spiritual terms" that are not, at the same time, Romantic terms.

The most characteristic difference between the idea-dominated Romantic poem and its idealized but non-Romantic predecessors lies in the perceived status of the idealizations. In a Romantic poem the realm of the ideal is always observed as precarious—liable to vanish or move beyond one's reach at any time. Central Romantic poems like "Ode to a Nightingale" or "La Belle Dame Sans Merci" typify this situation in the Romantic poem, which characteristically haunts, as Geoffrey Hartman has observed, borderlands and liminal territories. These are Romantic places because they locate areas of contradiction, conflict, and problematic alternatives. In short, Romantic poems take up transcendent and ideal subjects because these subjects occupy areas of critical uncertainty. The aim of the Romantic poem—especially in its early or "High Romantic" phases—is to rediscover the ground of stability in these situations. Later Romantic poems will often adopt a different procedure and attack the early Romantic terms of solution with the merciless critical razors of their despair.

All this contrasts sharply with Sidney's sonnet "Leave me O Love," which is a poem very much committed to transcendentals, and to defining a solution to its represented problems in ideal terms. The difference lies in the poem's unquestioning acceptance of a stable conceptual frame of reference in which its problems can be taken up and explored. In Romantic poems that frame of reference is precisely what stands at issue. I suppose it is unnecessary to recall here that the sonnet's unselfconscious acceptance of a traditional ideology does not prevent the work from developing its own special tensions, or from revealing those complex irresolutions which recur in human experience.

These sorts of differential are everywhere apparent in the corpus of literary works which we inherit. The great Medieval religious lyric "Lullay, lullay litel child"[11] is hardly less pitiful or forthright in its understanding of the world's cruelty and fundamental injustice than similar poems we know from Blake's *Songs of Innocence and of Experience.* But the Medieval lyric is not at all troubled *at the level of ideology* by such cruelty and injustice. Blake observes in the world's "Marks of weakness, marks of woe" a set of ideological contradictions which brings into question the entire structure of ideas which underpin his culture. This is why Blake takes up his subjects in a spirit of critical inquiry. Not so the Medieval lyric, however, which attempts to deal with the untrustworthiness of the world and human life at a more functional and existential level. This procedure is epitomized in the lyric's simple generic character—a cradle song to comfort a crying infant—which is based upon an accepted and traditional set of Christian virtues, concepts, and mythologies. The procedure is what makes the poem at once a simple lullaby and a parabolic representation of human life as a Christian trial and pilgrimage which extends from the cradle to the grave.

These sorts of distinction can and must be made even with problematic earlier writers like Donne, whose probing and skeptical intelligence is not, however, Romantic in character. When he declares that "new Philosophy calls all in doubt" ("The First Anniversary," 205) his attitude is at least as close to the anonymous author of "Lullay, lullay, litel child" as it is to Byron.

> And new Philosophy calls all in doubt,
> The Element of fire is quite put out;
> The Sun is lost, and th'earth, and no mans wit
> Can well direct him where to looke for it.
> And freely men confesse that this world's spent,
> When in the Planets, and the Firmament
> They seeke so many new; they see that this
> Is crumbled out againe to his Atomies.
> 'Tis all in peeces, all cohaerence gone;
> All just supply, and all Relation:
> Prince, Subject, Father, Sonne, are things forgot,
> For every man alone thinkes he hath got
> To be a Phoenix, and that then can bee
> None of that kinde, of which he is, but hee.
> This is the worlds condition now, and now
> She that should all parts to reunion bow,
> She that had all Magnetique force alone,
> To draw, and fasten sundred parts in one;
> She whom wise nature had invented then
> When she observ'd that every sort of men
> Did in their voyage in this worlds Sea stray,
> And needed a new compasse for their way. . .
> Shee, shee is dead; shee's dead: when thou knowst
>   this,
> Thou knowst how lame a cripple this world is.
> And learn'st thus much by our Anatomy,
> That this worlds generall sickenesse doth not lie
> In any humour, or one certaine part;
> But as thou sawest it rotten at the heart. (205-42)[12]

Though the satire here is based upon a Medieval *contemptus mundi*, it has clearly advanced to a self-conscious sense of the immediate sources of corruption. Donne's poem throughout shows his awareness of the special marks of his own personal wickedness and the analogous spiritual corruptions of his period. This awareness is historical, true, but in a Plutarchian rather than an Enlightenment, Higher Critical, or Hegelian mode.

Elizabeth Drury's death therefore recapitulates the ancient curse and "generall sicknesse" of "man," but Donne's verse "Anatomie" goes on to show his sense that the particular death is as it were an epitome for Donne and his age.

> Her death hath taught us dearely, that thou art
> Corrupt and mortall in thy purest part. (61-2)

Even the world's purest creature is subject to death and decay, Donne's rather mordant wit tells us. This is of course an ancient lesson and Donne knows it very well, nor has he ever doubted it. But he has been liable to forget it, like most people, and so Elizabeth Drury's death reminds him of it just as Donne's poem goes on to remind the reader. The poem develops its special personal force not from a Romantic self-consciousness about the grounds of human knowledge but from Donne's self-critical irony that he has needed so extreme a lesson to reteach him what he knew very well all along. Donne's criticism, as well as his related "Anatomie," is directed at himself for his worldliness, indeed, at the very nature of worldliness as he observes it anew in himself and his culture. But Donne does not question his culture's inherited grounds of judgment for the very reason that he does not see those grounds as culturally determined. To Donne, the world's corruption (including his own) and the blessedness of heaven (the communion of the saints) are not matters of ideology, they are matters of fact and truth.

All this is quite different from anything we shall find in any Romantic poem which has developed a comparable level of *critical* (as opposed to imaginative) intensity. The sheer force of the following lines at no point shatters the ideology which has made their expression possible.

> Shee, shee is dead; shee's dead; when thou knowst this,
> Thou knowst how drie a Cinder this world is.
> And learn'st thus much by our Anatomy,
> That 'tis in vaine to dew, or mollifie
> It with thy teares, or sweat, or blood: nothing

Is worth our travaile, griefe, or perishing,
But those rich joyes, which did possesse her heart,
Of which she's now partaker, and a part.

Compare this with the following stanzas from Canto IV of
Childe Harold's Pilgrimage, where the expressive intensity
matches Donne's lines, but where the force of that expression
takes its origin from an implacable nihilism.

121

Oh Love! no habitant of earth thou art—
An unseen seraph, we believe in thee,
A faith whose martyrs are the broken heart,
But never yet hath seen, nor e'er shall see
The naked eye, thy form, as it should be;
The mind hath made thee, as it peopled heaven,
Even with its own desiring phantasy,
And to a thought such shape and image given,
As haunts the unquench'd soul—parch'd—
    wearied—wrung—and riven.

122

Of its own beauty is the mind diseased,
And fevers into false creation:—where,
Where are the forms the sculptor's soul hath seized?—
In him alone. Can Nature show so fair?
Where are the charms and virtues which we dare
Conceive in boyhood and pursue as men,
The unreach'd Paradise of our despair,
Which o'er-informs the pencil and the pen,
And overpowers the page where it would bloom again?

123

Who loves, raves—'t is youth's frenzy; but the cure
Is bitterer still; as charm by charm unwinds
Which robed our idols, and we see too sure
Nor worth nor beauty dwells from out the mind's
Ideal shape of such; yet still it binds
The fatal spell, and still it draws us on,
Reaping the whirlwind from the oft-sown winds;

> The stubborn heart, its alchemy begun,
> Seems ever near the prize,—wealthiest when most
> undone.

This ferocity of statement winds on through several more stanzas, only to be interrupted by a brief pause to assert a commitment not to give over such a mode of thought and speech (stanza 127). Indeed, the whole of *Childe Harold's Pilgrimage* is determined to repeat this sort of verse, and therein lies its greatness. The level of Byron's hostility and frustration is such that it is only arbitrarily containable, even by himself. "The unreach'd Paradise of our despair": that complex oxymoron fixes the character of Byron's destructive—and self-destructive—thought. But even as we recognize a radical divergence between Byron and Donne in the level or status of their critical visions, we must not be misled to think that the force or intensity of Byron's expression is any greater than Donne's. Both are characteristically poets of unusual force and expressive vigor. They differ not in the intensity of their verse but in the special character which the intensity assumes. That character is in each case a function of sharp differences in their personal, political, cultural, and historical circumstances.

Let me conclude this part of the essay with a final set of contrasts which seem peculiarly apposite: between the Romantic literary ballad and the ballad of tradition.[13] The case of "La Belle Dame Sans Merci" is especially interesting because the poem makes such a conscious effort at imitation. This fact about the poem is evident from its first publication in Hunt's periodical *The Indicator*, where it was simply signed—with amused and amusing insolence—"Caviare." The self-consciousness with which Keats initially held back his name only increases one's awareness of the imitative character of the ballad. Consequently, like Keats's initial readers, we always begin a reading of the ballad with an implicit historical self-consciousness, and criticism must come to grips with that fact. So, if the critic does not understand, to start with, that this is a literary ballad (with all that such a term entails); and if he does not remember that it is a literary ballad written at a very specific period in England; and if, further, he neglects to take account of the fact that it was written by John Keats at a certain crucial moment in his life; well, critical analysis of the poem, without such knowledge, has nowhere to go. The fact that the poem makes an artistic pretense to anonymity—that this explicit fiction is part of its poetic aims—cannot begin to be understood outside the biographical context it pretends to have eliminated. The effect of the poem's "anonymity," that is, depends upon our realizing that it was in fact written by Keats.

If the personal dimension of Keats's poem is reinforced by its fictional pretense to anonymity, the more broadly historical context emphasizes, in a reciprocal way, the special quality of the subject Keats has chosen to write about. For a reader in 1819, this material will necessarily be received within the framework of a primitive anthropological perspective. The poem enters the world as a social act mediated by the previous history of the ballad revival, along with the complex and widespread critical discussion which surrounded that event. This specifically literary set of phenomena, it should be pointed out, is itself only a special instance of a general historical pattern observable throughout the ideological environment of Romantic culture.

The poem's materials, then, are necessarily taken to be fictive: though they come down to us via history, such materials reflect events which Keats and his readers do not really believe ever occurred in "objective" or outer history. Elfin ladies are mythological, her cave and its contents are drawn from magical traditions, the knight himself is part of a quasi-mythological romance tradition. The vision of the dead "pale kings and princes" is also drawn from what Keats had earlier ridiculed as "Vulgar Superstition," though in this case Keats does not write about such materials "In Disgust."

In short, the poem is plainly written by a person once described by a friend of his as a member "of the skeptical and republican school,"[14] and the work presupposes a like-minded audience. Its very appearance in Hunt's *Indicator* emphasizes these aspects of the poem and its audience. That it represents a "serious" discussion of superstitious and mythological material is equally plain, but the special quality of that seriousness cannot even begin to be defined if we do not see how self-conscious the poem expects its audience to be about its "fanciful" subject matter. We read the poem always aware that it is a fiction, and that it is given to us *as* a fiction (in contrast, for example, to *Beowulf,* or to the Gospels, or to any number of Medieval stories and ballads which are not presented *as* fictions, even though we now know that they are *in fact* using fictional materials). Keats requests his readers—as Coleridge did in "The Rime of the Ancient Mariner"—willingly to suspend their disbelief in such materials and enter, for a time, a fanciful space.

The important theoretical point to keep in mind here is that this entire situation only comes about because Keats's poetic materials are self-consciously recognized to be socially and historically defined. Romantic imagination emerges with the birth of an historical sense, which places the poet, and then the reader, at a critical distance from the poem's materials. The ballad's powerfully evoked mood of *melancholia* is the emotional sign of its central theme: that the emergence of an historical sense is marked by signs of division, by a whole dialectic of separations which operate between the poles of sympathy and criticism.

The reader's and critic's relation to a poem like "Thomas the Rhymer" (commonly so called)[15] is naturally quite different, for although we must read it across a self-conscious historical gap, we do not ascribe a similar self-consciousness to the original work. The traditional ballad's force, so far as a later reader is concerned, derives from its lack of self-consciousness. It seems strange to us because it does not seem strange to itself, as we see in the easy relations which prevail between the mortal Thomas and the Queen of Elfland.

> Syne they came on to a garden green,
>   And she pu'd an apple frae a tree—
> "Take this for thy wages, true Thomas;
>   It will give thee the tongue that can never lie."
>
> "My tongue is mine ain," true Thomas said;
>   "A gudely gift ye wad gie to me!
> I neither dought to buy nor sell,
>   As fair or tryst where I may be.
>
> "I dought neither speak to prince or peer,
>   Nor ask of grace from fair ladye."
> "Now hold thy peace!" the lady said,
>   "For as I say, so must it be."

By contrast, the balladeer and the knight-at-arms in Keats's poem are equally estranged persons: the knight by virtue of his experience with the elfin lady, and the balladeer by virtue of his narration of that experience. The latter-day ballad's Romantic agony focuses on the irrevocable loss of an entire area of significant human experience, as well as on the equally irrevocable loss of the meaning of that experience. The traditional ballad is marked by neither, a fact which, recognized by Keats, only heightens his poem's sense of estrangement.

"La Belle Dame Sans Merci" owes a partial but direct debt to the old ballad of "Thomas the Rhymer." Keats's poem draws upon Scott's presentation of the original ballad in his *Minstrelsy of the Scottish Border*, where the old text appears along with two other ballads: one is a redaction "from the ancient prophecies," and the other is Scott's frank imitation, a literary ballad which "continues" the story of Thomas to his departure from this world. These three poems together represent the process of historical displacement which Keats's ballad will later incorporate and push to an even greater extreme of self-consciousness. Scott's presentation lacks altogether the agonized intensity of Keats's ballad because Scott interposes between himself and his materials the objective eye of the editor and the philologist. These roles, assumed by Scott, permit him to experience and understand his materials without an extreme sense of displacement and estrangement. His view is ideologically Enlightened. Keats's poem, on the other hand, will not rest satisfied with Scott's historicism. Every part of Keats's ballad exhibits the restlessness and probing interrogations which Swingle has observed in typical Romantic poems. We shall later explore the critical significance of such Romantic works. For now we have merely to note, on the one hand, the extremity of the poem's Romanticism—in contrast, for example, to a literary ballad like "The Rime of the Ancient Mariner"; and, on the other, the gulf which separates Keats's ballad from its precedent models and analogues.

8

Wordsworth

and the Ideology of Romantic Poems

At this point we can return to consider in greater detail the problem of ideology in Romantic poems. In my reconsideration of Swingle's arguments I tried to put the subject matter of poetry back into the general aesthetic field of a poem's operation. The advantage of such a move, from the point of view of critical method, is that it supplies the critic with more ways for defining the special character of poetic works. The critic need not feel obliged to work within the narrow limits of a poem's purely linguistic elements. To take up the subject of poetry's conceptual and ideological elements is to allow criticism once again to intersect with those other traditional fields of inquiry so long alienated from the center of our discipline: textual criticism, bibliography, book production and distribution, reception history. On all fronts the critic will move to enlarge the concept of the poetical work beyond that of a special kind of linguistic system, beyond even a certain type of semiological structure. The critic will be asked to expand the concept of the poem-as-text to the poem as a more broadly based cultural product: in short, to the poem as poetical work. This hardly means that we cease being interested in the linguistic and semiological aspects of poems; rather, it simply entails that those matters will be taken up in a cultural context which is at once more comprehensive (theoretically) and more particular (socially and historically).[16]

These general considerations lead us to conclude, then, that the "Isms" of Romantic poetry should not be set aside when we come to study Romantic poems. On the contrary, certain features which are peculiar to poems from the Romantic Period make it crucial to pay attention to those "Isms." I want now to consider two of the most important of these features. The patterns I shall be marking out are widespread in the works of the period. I shall concentrate here on Wordsworth, however, because his works—like his position in the Romantic Movement—are normative and, in every sense, exemplary.

We begin by forcing the critical act to attend to the specific referential patterns which appear in specific poems. These references may be factual or cognitive, but in all cases they will be historically and socially specific. In the case of Romantic poems, we shall find that the works tend to develop different sorts of artistic means with which to occlude and disguise their own involvement in a certain nexus of historical relations. This act of evasion, as it were, operates most powerfully whenever the poem is most deeply immersed in its cognitive (i.e., its ideological) materials and commitments. For this reason the critic of Romantic poetry must make a determined effort to elucidate the subject matter of such poems *historically*: to define the specific ways in which certain stylistic forms intersect and join with certain factual and cognitive points of reference.

Rather than speak of the method in such general terms any longer, however, let me commence with "The Ruined Cottage,"[17] partly because it is a great poem, and partly because its structural methods for dealing with substantive issues are so clear. In his Fenwick note Wordsworth says that the work was based upon incidents and conditions which he had himself observed in 1793 in the southwest of England. The information is to an extent supererogatory since no one reading the story when it was first published in 1814, still less if it had been read earlier in a manuscript version, would have been unaware of the context in which the tragic events are embedded.

Margaret's husband Robert is a weaver and the poem focuses upon the precarious state in which this cottage industry found itself in the late eighteenth and early nineteenth century. Two bad harvests coupled with "that worse affliction . . . the plague of war" (136) bring Robert's family to the point of ruin, as he becomes one among those "shoals of artizans" who

> Were from their daily labor turned away
> To hang for bread on parish charity,
> They and their wives and children. (154-7)

Eventually Robert joins the army in a pathetically imcompetent and misplaced effort to free his family from their economic plight. Robert disappears in the gulf of war while his wife and child are left to the beautiful slow-motion narrative of their painfully slow-motion demise.

I have myself re-narrated these well-known details because the strategy of Wordsworth's poem is to elide their distinctiveness from our memories, to drive the particulars of this tragedy to a region that is too deep either for tears or for what Wordsworth here calls "restless thoughts" (198). Margaret's cottage is gradually overgrown and "ruined" when "Nature" invades its neglected precincts. This—the poem's dominant and most memorable process—finally comes to stand as an emblem of the endurance of Nature's care and ceaseless governance, just as it glances obliquely at the pathetic incompetence of individual, cultural, and institutional efforts to give stability to human affairs. Not England, not Robert's social and economic institutions, not even Robert by himself can afford protection against "A time of trouble." Margaret's cottage will collapse under their "neglect," which Wordsworth sees as inevitable, indeed, as a function of the social *rerum natura*.

This gradual collapse of the cottage into what Wordsworth calls, in his characteristic form of Romantic wit, Nature's "silent overgrowings" (506), has yet another analogue, however, in the poem's narrative method itself. To read Wordsworth's re-telling of this pitiful story is to be led further and further from a clear sense of the historical origins and circumstantial causes of Margaret's tragedy. The place of such thoughts and such concerns is usurped, overgrown. Armytage, poet, and reader all fix their attention on a gathering mass of sensory, and chiefly vegetable, details. Hypnotized at this sensational surface, the light of sense goes out and "The secret spirit of humanity" emerges.

> I stood, and leaning o'er the garden gate
> Reviewed that Woman's suff'rings; and it seemed
> To comfort me while with a brother's love
> I blessed her in the impotence of grief.
> At length towards the cottage I returned
> Fondly, and traced with milder interest,
> That secret spirit of humanity
> Which, 'mid the calm oblivious tendencies

> Of nature, 'mid her plants, her weeds and flowers,
> And silent overgrowings, still survived.
> The old man seeing this resumed, and said,
> "My Friend, enough to sorrow have you given,
> The purposes of wisdom ask no more:
> Be wise and chearful, and no longer read
> The forms of things with an unworthy eye.
> She sleeps in the calm earth, and peace is here.
>   (497-512)

Margaret's devotion, love, and fidelity to her house speak to Wordsworth's "restless" narrator from beyond the grave and transfer his allegiance from "The Party of Humanity" to its secret spiritual replacement. "The Ruined Cottage" aims to effect a similar translation of attention and commitments in the reader:

> I well remember that those very plumes,
> Those weeds, and the high spear-grass on that wall,
> By mist and silent rain-drops silvered o'er,
> As once I passed, did to my mind convey
> So still an image of tranquility,
> So calm and still, and looked so beautiful
> Amid the uneasy thoughts which filled my mind,
> That what we feel of sorrow and despair
> From ruin and from change, and all the grief
> The passing shews of being leave behind,
> Appeared an idle dream that could not live
> Where meditation was. I turned away,
> And walked along my road in happiness." (513-24)

"The Ruined Cottage" is an exemplary case of what commentators mean when they speak of the "displacement" that occurs in a Romantic poem. An Enlightenment mind like Diderot's or Godwin's or Crabbe's would study this poem's events in social and economic terms, but Wordsworth is precisely interested in preventing—in actively countering—such a focus of concentration. The displacement is reproduced in the poem's subtle transformation of Wordsworth's 1793-4 world—including the social and political discontents which dominated his life at that time—into the changed world of

1797-8, when he began to write the poem in the exuberant atmosphere of Racedown and Alfoxden. Wordsworth himself becomes a poetic narrator, and the focus of his original feelings of dislocation are displaced from France and the Bishop of Llandaff to the more homely and immediate discomforts of the walking tourist (lines 18-26). In such circumstances, the story of Margaret produces in the narrator a sense of shame and humility before a great suffering, and an overflow of sympathy and love for the sufferer rather than, as in 1793-4, a sense of outrage, and an overflow of angry judgment upon those whom Wordsworth at the time held accountable for helping to maintain the social conditions which generated a surplus of social evil.

I shall have more to say about the poetic significance of these erasures and displacements in a later part of this essay. Here I am interested in the fact of the displacement, and in the extent to which—including the manner in which—it is brought about. In works like "The Ruined Cottage" and the Salisbury Plain poems we are kept in a direct contact with the particular social circumstances with which these works are concerned. Nevertheless, James Butler is right to say that "*The Ruined Cottage* is not a work of social protest,"[18] a fact about the poem which appears in the process of attenuation which I have been remarking upon. Yet the character and extent of the displacement in "The Ruined Cottage" is quite different—is far less extreme—from what we may observe in "Tintern Abbey."

Here the temporal displacement is at once more exact and yet less clear, more specific and yet not so easy to understand. The "Five Years" of which the poem speaks delimit on the one hand Wordsworth's trip to Salisbury Plain and North Wales in the summer of 1793, and on the other his return visit, particularly to the abbey, on July 13, 1798. In the course of the poem not a word is said about the French Revolution, or about the impoverished and dislocated country poor, or—least of all—that this event and these conditions might be structurally related to each other. All these are matters which had been touched upon, however briefly, in "The Ruined Cottage," but in "Tintern Abbey" they are further displaced out of the narrative.

But not entirely displaced. As in "The Ruined Cottage," these subjects are present in the early parts of the poem, only to be completely erased after line 23. But their presence is maintained in such an oblique way that readers—especially later scholars and interpreters—have passed them by almost without notice. Recently Marjorie Levinson, in a brilliantly researched and highly controversial polemic, has redrawn our attention to the importance of the date in the subtitle, and to the special significance which Tintern Abbey and its environs had for an informed English audience of the period.[19] Her argument is complex and detailed and neither can nor need be rehearsed here. Suffice it to say—and to see—that Wordsworth situates his poem (and his original experience) on the eve of Bastille Day. Secondly, the force of lines 15-23 depends upon our knowing that the ruined abbey had been in the 1790s a favorite haunt of transients and displaced persons—of beggars and vagrants of various sorts, including (presumably) "female vagrants." Wordsworth observes the tranquil orderliness of the nearby "pastoral farms" and draws these views into a relation with the "vagrant dwellers in the houseless woods" of the abbey. This relation contains a startling, even a shocking, contrast of social conditions. Even more, it suggests an ominous social and economic fact of the period: that in 1793 no great distance separated the houseless vagrant from the happy cottager, as "The Ruined Cottage" made so painfully clear. Much of Wordsworth's poem rests on the initial establishment of this bold image of contradiction, on the analogous one hinted at in the subtitle's date, and on the relation between them which the poem subtly encourages us to make. It was, of course, a relation which Wordsworth himself made explicit in his *Letter to the Bishop of Llandaff*.

But like "The Ruined Cottage," "Tintern Abbey"'s method is to replace an image and landscape of contradiction with one dominated by "the power/ Of harmony" (48-9). So in 1798 he observes the ruined abbey and its environs "with an eye made quiet" by such power. He sees not "the landscape [of] a blind man's eye" (25)—not the place of conflict and contradiction which he now associates with his own "blind" jacobinism of 1793—but an earlier, more primal landscape which he explicitly associates with his childhood. This last is the landscape which does not fill the eye of the mind with external and soulless images, but with "forms of beauty" (24) through which we can "see into the life of things" (50), to penetrate the surface of a landscape to reach its indestructible heart and meaning:

> a sense sublime
> Of something far more deeply interfused,
> Whose dwelling is the light of setting suns,
> And the round ocean, and the living air,
> And the blue sky, and in the mind of man,
> A motion and a spirit, that impels
> All thinking things, all objects of all thought,
> And rolls through all things. (96-103)

This famous passage defines Wordworth's sense of "the life of things" which lies beneath the external "forms of beauty." The lines have transcended ordinary description altogether, however, and replaced what might have been a picture *in* the mind (of a ruined abbey) with a picture *of* the mind: a picture, that is—as the pun on the preposition makes clear—of the "mind" in its act of generating itself within an external landscape. Wordsworth narrates that act of replacement in four magnificent lines of verse:

> And now, with gleams of half-extinguish'd thought,
> With many recognitions dim and faint,
> And somewhat of a sad perplexity,
> The picture of the mind revives again. (59-62)

The abbey associated with 1793 fades, as in a palimpsest, and in its disappearing outlines we begin to discern not a material reality but a process, or power, exercising itself in an act of sympathy which is its most characteristic feature. No passage in Wordsworth better conveys the actual moment when a spiritual displacement occurs—when the light and appearances of sense fade into an immaterial plane of reality, the landscape of Wordsworth's emotional needs.

That Wordsworth was himself well aware of what his poem was doing is clear from the conclusion, where he declares himself to be a "worshipper of Nature" (153) rather than a comunicant in some visible church. Whereas these fade and fall to ruin, the abbey of the mind suffers no decay, but passes from sympathetic soul to sympathetic soul—here, through all the phases of Wordsworth's own changing life, and thence from him to Dorothy as well, whose mind:

Shall be a mansion for all lovely forms,
Thy memory be as a dwelling-place
For all sweet sounds and harmonies; oh! then
If solitude, or fear, or pain, or grief,
Should be thy portion, with what healing thoughts
Of tender joy wilt thou remember me,
And these my exhortations!   (140-46)

Dorothy is, of course, the reader's surrogate just as Tintern Abbey's ruins appear, on the one hand, as a visible emblem of everything that is transitory, and on the other as an emotional focus of all that is permanent.

At the poem's end we are left only with the initial scene's simplest natural forms: "these steep woods and lofty cliffs,/ And this green pastoral landscape" (158-9). Everything else has been erased—the abbey, the beggars and displaced vagrants, all that civilized culture creates and destroys, gets and spends. We are not permitted to remember 1793 and the turmoil of the French Revolution, neither its 1793 hopes nor—what is more to the point for Wordsworth—the subsequent ruin of those hopes. Wordsworth displaces all that into a spiritual economy where disaster is self-consciously transformed into the threat of disaster ("*If* this/ Be but a vain belief," 50-51; my italics), and where that threat, fading into a further range of self-conscious anticipation, suddenly becomes a focus not of fear but of hope. For the mind has triumphed over its times.

Thus the poem concludes in what appears to be an immense gain, but what is in reality the deepest and most piteous loss. Between 1793 and 1798 Wordsworth lost the world merely to gain his own immortal soul. The greatness of this great poem lies in the clarity and candor with which it dramatizes not merely this event, but the structure of this event.

This part of my argument can be briefly concluded. The processes of elision which I have been describing reach their notorious and brilliant apogee in the "Intimations Ode," a work which has driven the philologically inclined critic to despair. In this poem all contextual points of reference are absorbed back into the poem's intertextual structure. The famous "pansy at my feet," the one tree of many, the timely utterance: readers have sought long and in vain to specify the references of these passages. Perhaps we glimpse a metaphoric afterimage of the Bastille in "Shades of the prison-house"—but perhaps not. The poem generalizes—we now like to say mythologizes—all its conflicts, or rather resituates those conflicts out of a socio-historical context and into an ideological one. "We in thought will join your throng." This is the famous process of internalization which is at once the ode's central problem and its final solution as well.

The problem is clearly presented in stanza IV when Wordsworth acknowledges his belief that "all the earth is gay" (29)

> Oh evil day! if I were sullen
> While Earth herself is adorning,
> This sweet May-morning,
> And the Children are culling
> On every side,
> In a thousand valleys far and wide,
> Fresh flowers; while the sun shines warm,
> And the Babe leaps up on his Mother's arm:—
> I hear, I hear, with joy I hear! (42-50)

The pattern in the first four stanzas is to set a contrast between all that Wordsworth can "hear," which the poem associates with his belief in and feelings of universal joy, and all that Wordsworth can and cannot see. These latter things, which Wordsworth associates initially with loss, induce in him a sense of fear and anxiety. The contrast establishes a distinction between a world of the indefinite and the unseen on the one hand, and a world of visible particulars on the other. "The things which I have seen I now can see no more"; the catalogue in stanza II is itself not a record of immediacies, but a recitation of generalities recalled from particular past experiences, as the very heterogeneous character of the items shows. And the unadorned presentation of these memory-mediated particulars explains that the flight of the visionary gleam is a function of the loss of immediacy.

In short, the poem's problem emerges when Wordsworth recognizes that his sense of a universal joy—his insight into the life of things—has resulted in his loss of the concrete and particular:

> —But there's a Tree, of many, one,
> A single Field which I have looked upon,

> Both of them speak of something that is gone:
> The Pansy at my feet
> Doth the same tale repeat. (51-5)

Scholars who have labored to identify that tree and the "single field," and to locate the spot where Wordsworth observed the pansy, have followed the poet's own futile quest. These things are gone, and Wordsworth fears—despite his own reiterated convictions—that their departure will signal the passage of "the glory and the dream" as well.

As "The Ruined Cottage" and "Tintern Abbey" have already shown, the disappearance of such particulars occurred as part of a strategy of displacement. But where these earlier poems involved dramatizations and enactments of the strategy's discovery, the "Intimations Ode" is a study of its character and, finally, a justification and embodiment of its operations. The ode begins with a fearful sense that the immediate and concrete experience has disappeared into the mists of consciousness and memory. It concludes, however, with the reiterated conviction that

> The thought of our past years in me doth breed
> Perpetual benediction. (134-5)

Immediacy is "fugitive" and impermanent, but not so the consciousness of all that is fugitive. Wordsworth therefore lifts a final "song of thanks and praise" for the activity of displacement itself, for the moments of loss. In the ode, objective history has disappeared. The poem annihilates its history, biographical and socio-historical alike, and replaces these particulars with a record of pure consciousness. The paradox of the work is that it embodies an immediate and concrete experience of that most secret and impalpable of all human acts: the transformation of fact into idea, and of experience into ideology.

Its pathos is a function of that paradox. For Wordsworth's poem does not actually transcend the evils it is haunted by, it merely occupies them at the level of consciousness. That Wordsworth's is as well a false consciousness needs scarcely to be said, nor is it an indictment of the poem's greatness that this should be the case. The work completes and perfects the tragic losses of Wordsworth's life and times. Had he merely "yielded up moral questions in despair" (*Prelude* XI, 305) his case would have been pitiful. Wordsworth went on to struggle further with those problems and to arrive at what he believed was their solution. What he actually discovered was no more than his own desperate need for a solution. The reality of that need mirrored a cultural one that was much greater and more widespread. Wordsworth transformed both of these realities into illusions. The process began with the displacement of the problem inwardly, but when he went on to conceptualize his need, as we observe in the ode, the pity of Wordsworth's situation approaches tragic proportions. Indeed, it is a very emblem of the tragedy of his epoch, for in that conceptualization Wordsworth imprisoned his true voice of feeling within the bastille of his consciousness. Wordsworth made a solitude and he called it peace.

Poetry like Wordsworth's belongs to what Hans Enzensberger has called "The Consciousness Industry"[20]—a light industry, if the pun be permitted, which Wordsworth and the other Romantics helped to found, and which they sought to preserve free of cultural contamination. The futility of this effort is apparent in the curricula of our educational institutions. When we read and study Wordsworth we always do so within a certain institutional framework—for good and ill alike. Because we must come to grips with this social dimension of "Wordsworth's poetry", one word more remains to be said.

"Like a planet revolving around an absent sun, an ideology is made out of what it does not mention; it exists because there are things which must not be spoken of."[21] These remarks are a latter-day version of a recurrent truth. From Wordsworth's vantage, an ideology is born out of things which (literally) *cannot* be spoken of. So the "Immortality Ode" is crucial for us because it speaks about ideology from the point of view and in the context of its origins. If Wordsworth's poetry elides history, we observe in this "escapist" or "reactionary" move its own self-revelation. It is a rare, original, and comprehensive record of the birth and character of a particular ideology—in this case, one that has been incorporated into our academic programs. The idea that poetry, or even consciousness, can set one free of the ruins of history and culture is the grand illusion of every Romantic poet. This idea continues as one of the most important shibboleths of our culture, especially—and naturally—at its higher levels.

Wordsworth stands to his later history as a poetic tale stands to its forms of worship. To his earlier history he stands as a prophet in his own country. Understanding this historical distinction is an imperative of literary criticism, for it is a distinction which enables poetry to be read as part of a society and its culture—without at the same time being absorbed by those structures. It is a distinction, as well, which Blake observed when he differentiated "men" from what he wittily called "the states" which they passed through. Indeed, when criticism begins to set poetry "free" in this manner—that is to say, when criticism restores poetry to its historical determinations—it will have begun to set itself "free" as well. The works of the Romantic Period are not in bondage to themselves: they survive in the valley of their saying, where they speak their truths (including the errors of their truths). Rather, they have been mastered by a critical history which has come to possess them in the name of various Romanticisms. Swingle's acute sense of this event leads him to seek a non-ideological approach to Romantic works. But this move is futile, not merely because ideology is a central (as opposed to a "supporting") factor in Romantic works, but also because it is a central factor in the criticism of Romantic works. The issue now is whether critics shall be able to distinguish themselves and their works from the "states" which they too inhabit and serve.

PART III

Cassandra's Gift:
Romantic Poems and
the Critique of Ideology

9

Coleridge, "Kubla Kahn,"

and the Later Poetry

Heine's approach to Romantic works is a criticism which began to set those works free of their own inherent limitations, on the one hand, and from their openness to a subsequent ideological appropriation on the other. Heine's criticism, that is to say, represents an alternative to Romantic self-representation or repetition (e.g., Coleridge's criticism, or Harold Bloom's) and Hegelian possession (which dominates, in various forms, the present scholarly community). Heine's criticism is therefore a useful model, particularly at this historical juncture.

The distinctive advance represented by this criticism, however, does not lie so much in the exposure of the limits of Romanticism as it does in the capacity for self-criticism. Heine's uneasy relation to various European cultural and political institutions parallels his lifelong pursuit of ideological independence. He was a man who was well aware of the various states he passed through, some of which have distinct names: Germany, France, Romanticism, Christianity, Judaism. What we need to recall, at this point, is that Heine learned his critical procedures partly from studying the works of the Romantic authors, where he observed various heroic acts of self-criticism. Heine learned self-criticism partly from the very writers and works he came to place under judgment.

What Heine discovered in writers like Uhland, Hoffmann, Chamisso, and Tieck, students of English Romanticism may observe as well in the writers they study. Few experiences are more moving than to read some of Coleridge's later poems, particularly if one does so in the context of his later works in prose. *The Statesman's Manual* appeared in 1816, *Aids to Reflection* in

1825, and *On the Constitution of Church and State* in 1830, but as the Sage of Highgate delivered these works of spiritual and social ideology to the clerisy he helped to create, he was also writing a number of brief but disturbing poetical works. Between 1825 and 1830 Coleridge drafted such poems and fragments as "The Pang More Sharp Than All," "Phantom or Fact," "Self-Knowledge," and "Love's Apparition and Evanishment." The fact that these works are all structurally related to what Coleridge specifically called the first and last of them—that is, to allegory—underscores Coleridge's sense of the desperate subjects and attitudes they were dealing with.

To Coleridge, allegory was a poetical form which he associated[1] with a divided or alienated consciousness, and he himself resorted to it—most memorably, in his prose piece "Allegoric Vision"—to open a critical and self-conscious view of ideas and institutions. Allegory was not, for Coleridge, a poetic form appropriate to the One Life; rather, it was peculiarly adapted to expose and explore critically the world of illusions, divisions, and false-consciousness. Thus E. H. Coleridge observes of the shape-shifting appearances of Coleridge's original "Allegoric Vision":

> The "Allegoric Vision" dates from August, 1795. It served as a kind of preface or prologue to Coleridge's first Theological Lecture on "The Origin of Evil. The Necessity of Revelation deduced from the Nature of Man. An Examination and Defence of the Mosaic Dispensation." . . . The purport of these Lectures was to uphold the golden mean of Unitarian orthodoxy as opposed to the Church on the one hand, and infidelity or materialism on the other. "Superstition" stood for and symbolized the Church of England. Sixteen years later this opening portion of an unpublished Lecture was rewritten and printed in *The Courier* (Aug. 31, 1811), with the heading "An Allegoric Vision: Superstition, Religion, Atheism." The attack was now diverted from the Church of England to the Church of Rome. "Men clad in black robes," intent on gathering in their Tenths, become "men clothed in ceremonial robes, who with menacing countenances drag some reluctant victim to a vast idol, framed of iron bars intercrossed which formed at the same time an immense cage, and yet represented the form of a human Colossus. At the base of the statue

I saw engraved the words 'To Dominic holy and merciful, the preventer and avenger of Soul-murder'." The vision was turned into a political *jeu d'esprit* levelled at the aiders and abettors of Catholic Emancipation. . . . A third adaptation of the "Allegorical Vision" was affixed to the Introduction to *A Lay Sermon* . . . . which was published in 1817. The first fifty-six lines, which contain a description of Italian mountain scenery, were entirely new, but the rest of the "Vision" is an emended and softened reproduction to the preface to the Lecture of 1795. The moral he desires to point is the "falsehood of extremes."[2]

A most disturbing aspect of Coleridge's later "allegorical visions" is the fact that they are all self-absorbed and introspective works. In these poems Coleridge is not exploring politics, society, or the apparatuses and ideologies of the state, he is applying an allegorical deconstruction to what he himself saw as the most fundamental objects of the mind, the heart, and the soul itself.

Walter J. Bate has shrewdly asked us to recall, when reading these poems, that "Coleridge was familiar with such states" of spiritual desolation all his life.[3] Two of Coleridge's best known poems of spiritual aridity—"Limbo" and "Ne Plus Ultra"—were born and buried in his *Notebooks* in 1817, while perhaps the most impressive of all these pieces—"Constancy to an Ideal Object"—may have existed in some form as early as 1804, though it more probably belongs to 1817 or shortly thereafter. These dates are to be noted only because they emphasize an important pair of facts about Coleridge's poetry: first, that it was always subject to a negative dialectic of "apparition and evanishment"; and second, that this negative pattern grew more firmly rooted in the poetry even as Coleridge's prose developed a more confident and developed ideological focus. Bate has well said of the later poems "To Nature" and "Self-Knowledge":

Coleridge here [in "To Heaven"] abandons . . . his confidence that the constructions of imagination are revelations of truth, and he also posits a possible separation of nature from God. . . . A similar symbolic gesture . . . is located in . . . "Self Knowledge." Here again the symbolic gesture lies in the surrender—a giving up to God—of a jewel of Coleridge's intellectual crown, namely, his cherished maxim . . . *Know Thyself.*[4]

The feelings of desperation and bewilderment that emerge with these sorts of ideological losses and surrenders are powerful ^nd terribly moving precisely because their vehicular form is a ‾ᵈᵍᵉ shared with Wordsworth the conviction ᴛ ᴛʜe means for seeing into the life of things ᴜᴜ. The "Idea" so cherished by Coleridge was a ᴛ imperative of what he called the Reason, but it was ᴀᴜ apprehendable reality of what he called the poetic Imagination. Furthermore, and again the parallel with Wordsworth is clear, Coleridge's commitment to this Idea was always reciprocally related to his sense of the world as a field of loss, division, and betrayal. The Romantic subject of a poem like "Kubla Khan" is loss and the threat of loss. The stately pleasure dome is, as all commentators have pointed out, the most precarious of structures. Indeed, we only see it obliquely, and the closest thing we have to a direct view is of its shadow trembling on the (symbolic) river which flows through the Khan's equally precarious domain. The poem's central image of a civilization constructed on the pleasure principle is a gesture defying those "ancestral voices prophesying war." This Jerusalem of the Khan is a poetic dream, an Idea of the Reason imaginatively raised up against the barbarism of history along the stream of time, which threatens to carry all things "down to a sunless sea." The precariousness of the dream of a truly human civilization is emphasized by the fact that it is associated here with Kubla Khan, the notorious Tartar who brought the whole of China under his absolute control by military force.

Coleridge explicitly relates the story of Kubla Khan to the poetic principle—first, in the prose preface to the poem, where the subject of loss is also treated, and again in the second part of the lyric proper, where Coleridge calls up the possibility of a renewed imaginative vision. Like "Dejection: An Ode," "Kubla Khan" is most centrally threatened with the loss of the poetic faculty itself, which emerges as the poem's ultimate defense against the ancestral voices and the Khan as well.

In later poems like "To Nature" Coleridge dramatizes the extinction of his shaping imaginative spirit, his inability to revive in himself the song of the Abyssinian maid:

> In vain we supplicate the Powers above;
> There is no resurrection for the Love
> That, nursed in tenderest care, yet fades away
> In the chill'd heart by gradual self-decay. (29-32)

This is the poetry of a fearful conclusiveness, a statement poetry which transforms its poetic images from generative symbols into critical allegories. Of course, Coleridge's later poetry shows little loss in poetical power; what it demonstrates is the loss of his poetic beliefs. Coleridge's late imagination shapes the spirits of his nightmares: that the love, the knowledge, and the imagination which he has believed in are chimeras, at best momentary defenses against the world's ancestral violence and darkness. To judge the value of poems like "Constancy to an Ideal Object" and "Love's Apparition and Evanishment" we might well recall Wordsworth's similar revisionary poems. "Peele Castle" has been rightly called "a palinode"[5] to Wordsworth's earlier poetic faith, yet Wordsworth never wrote a greater lyric piece. That it is a poem of despair is not a measure of its poetic value but of its special ideological focus.

The major poetic difference between a poem like "Kubla Khan" and works such as "Constancy to an Ideal Object" is stylistic. The former is dominated by that typical Romantic device which has been called "surmise."[6] When we read toward the end of the poem:

> Could I revive within me
> Her sympathy and song,
> To such a deep delight 'twould win me,
> That with music loud and long,
> I would build that dome in air,   (42-46)

we do so in the context of lines 1-41 where the dome was raised up for us in the medium of verse and vision. Furthermore, we recall as well the poetic injunction imbedded in Coleridge's introductory prose narrative of loss: "Stay awhile/ . . . soon/ The visions will return." Coleridge's poem works at all points to sustain its own generative energy at the ideological level, and to drive out the fears which beset the mind of his poem. The surmise executed in lines 41-6 concludes, therefore, in an oblique fulfillment. We do not leave the poem with a vision of the pleasure dome, but we do leave it with an image which equally confirms the belief that visionary power has returned and will continue to do so.

> I would build that dome in air,
> That sunny dome! those caves of ice!
> And all who heard should see them there,
> And all should cry, Beware! Beware!
> His flashing eyes, his floating hair!
> Weave a circle round him thrice,
> And close your eyes with holy dread,
> For he on honey-dew hath fed,
> And drunk the milk of Paradise. (45-53)

The subjunctive "Could . . . would . . . should" has succeeded to a poetry a presence. Those who "should" hear the song and see the dome appear suddenly and address the reader with exclamations and a series of present imperatives. Thus the poem ends in a dramatic representation of imagination's own self-renovating powers. The poem is, as everyone agrees, about the poetical faculty itself, and the poem's central problem—that this faculty may lose its potency—is finally set aside in a set of gestures which show its continuous operation to the poem's end.

At this point we might pause to be certain that we are clear as to what is involved in a resolution of this sort. The poem's poetic excellence lies in the careful adaptation of its stylistic means to its ideological commitments and presuppositions. It is a poem about poetry, true, but more particularly it is a poem about a special ideology (Romantic) of poetic work. If you look at the poem from an aesthetic vantage you see the congruence of its operations, (the balance and reconciliation of opposite and discordant qualities) while from the conceptual side you observe the conclusive emotional affirmation of the ideology it sets out to reveal, interrogate, and finally confirm ("The visions will return"). The poem is not so much about poetry, then, as it is about Romantic poetry, and the special features of certain Romantic ideological pursuits (both stylistic and conceptual).

One important feature of Romantic ideology, as we have already seen, is the belief that poetical works can transcend historical divisions by virtue of their links with Imagination, through which we see into the permanent life of things. Central to this Romantic view is the idea that poetic vision is the *cor cordium*, the epipsyche, the final ground on which all other conceptual formations must depend, at least so far as human perceptions are concerned. In the case of a Romantic poem, then, to say that it is "about poetry" is tantamount to saying that it is about the ultimate grounds of knowledge and being. Horace's "Ars Poetica" is a great work, and it too is "about poetry", but clearly it has engaged with its subject from a very different vantage. Coleridge's poem is at once more desperate and more grandiose. Similarly, if we set "Kubla Khan" beside, say, *The Dunciad*, the difference is equally clear. No less passionate a work than "Kubla Khan," *The Dunciad* struggles against the threat of cultural degeneracy; unlike Pope, however, Coleridge's struggle is carried out in purely conceptual space. Pope is able to see his enemies, where Coleridge is forced to imagine them. Those prose persons from Porlock become, in the verse of the poem proper, the unnamed but fearful antagonists who have waged ancestral war against the equally fearful Khan. They are unnameable because they are legion: they are everything that works to destroy vision, at any time and in all places, and they include the Khan himself.

Ultimately, then, a poem like "Kubla Khan" operates through symbols because both its subject matter and its style are "ideal." The specific idea (historical) of such a poem is that poetry works at the level of final Ideas. Its concrete symbols deliberately forego any immediate social or cultural points of reference in order to engage with its audience at a purely conceptual level. Indeed, they engage specifically at the level of ideology, for the conceptual aspects of the poem are delivered obliquely and unselfconsciously, through symbols. The work compels a nonrational form of assent to a latent structure of ideas; in the end, it urges the reader to swear allegiance to the idea of non-rational and unselfconscious forms of knowing.

The excellence of Norman Rudich's political interpretation of "Kubla Khan" lies in his sure grasp of the poem's method of (what he calls) "mythopoeic" transformations. The work's immediate historical and social points of reference are all displaced into symbolic forms, and Rudich explains the mechanism of these displacements very well.

Mythopoeia has another function, an aesthetic one, to

raise the poet's vision to sublime heights, heroic gran-
duer. This is Coleridge's flight from the political realities
of his day metamorphosed into an heroic assault on the
bastions of human prejudice and delusion, with the
inspired poet leading the vanguard of enlightened spirits.
The truth of history is that political revolutions betrayed
by tyrants come and go, a bloody, repetitive succession
of disappointments. The poet alone can truly lead
mankind out of the infernal cycle and to the happiness
of spiritual peace in harmonious reconciliation with
himself and God's nature.

"Kubla Khan" has all the markings of Coleridge's
reactionary politics. Although it is directed against the
two Tartar despots, Kubla and Napoleon, Coleridge
links Bonapartist imperialism and the French Revolution in a single anathema. The poem is an exhortation
to abandon political struggle for the sake of the highest
cultivation of the aesthetic, moral, and religious qualities
of the soul. It separates poetry from history, sublimating
its meaning into the theological realms of absolute
Truth and eternal categories of Good and Evil.[7]

The commentary recapitulates the basic articles of Coleridge's
aesthetic and cultural beliefs, which "Kubla Khan" tests and
finally affirms. The Khan is the conqueror and master of the
world, but in Coleridge's view he is really no more than a passing historical representative cast up from the central "Romantic
chasm" at the root of the stream of time. The master of this historical potentate is the Idea which he embodies, and final
mastery lies with those who create and master the world of
Ideas: God, ultimately, but in the mortal sphere the manipula-
tors of the creative imagination.

"Kubla Khan" is a great Romantic poem which in the end
affirms Coleridge's basic ideology of poetry and the power of the
creative imagination. He believed that one could "not hope from
outward forms to win/ The passion and the life, whose fountains
are within"; in "Kubla Khan" that inward creative fountain is the
center of the Khan's domain and the source of its richness, and
the poem represents itself as the spontaneous expression of a
congruent inner vision. But the entire project of Imagination in
this poem is continually threatened and haunted by fearful

images of evil and destruction. The Khan's civilization has been fashioned with the sword and is destined to a similarly violent end. The deep Romantic chasm is at once holy and savage, the locus of the creative fountain but also a place associated with a "woman wailing for her demon lover."

The poem's central ideas, in other words, are as precarious as everything else in the poem, which seems to have generated simultaneously the images of its creation and the threat of its destruction. This conflict appears at the surface of the poem—in its images—but because the poem's ideology holds that these surfaces represent the apparition and aesthesis of the underlying Idea, the work haunts its own precincts with a fear that its genius may be a demon or a tyrant, and its paradise an illusion (or worse). Consequently, the poem maintains its affirmative stance by forcing itself to live under the threat of its own destruction, and in fear of the possibility that its beliefs are rank illusions. The idea of the creative imagination in "Kubla Khan" is therefore properly associated with a powerful tyrant, though he is a benevolent and well-meaning one.

The poem's greatness does not, however, lie in its ideology as such. The ideological affirmations localize a set of emotional tensions and contradictions which appear in the course of the poem. The affirmations are important for criticism not in themselves—not for their Truth-value—but because they are part of the poem's specific human content—for their truth-value. Criticism cannot set the poem's ideas aside as mere enabling devices or peripheral matters. A poem's ideas are crucial to criticism because the tensions in the poetry emerge when the ideas are affirmed (or questioned or even rejected). This is the case with all poetry. In a Romantic poem like "Kubla Khan," however, an additional emphasis is placed upon the poem's conceptual investments, since the central Idea toward which the imagination gestures is a place of ultimate resort. The fear which plays all about "Kubla Khan" is a displaced critical reaction toward the poem's ideological commitments and (unselfconscious) affirmations. As in so much of Wordsworth's poetry, "Kubla Khan" accepts a ministry of fear as a fair price to pay for its imaginative resolutions. This acceptance is also part of its ideology. The emotional conflicts which are generated as a consequence, however, form the structure of that more comprehensive emotional revelation which the poem finally achieves at the level of self-consciousness: that is to say, at the level of a critical (rather than an ideological) response.

Coleridge's central ideas, then, are an integral part of a poem like "Kubla Khan," whose emotional structures are only elaborated through the play and interrelationships between the poem's surface images and its underlying ideas. The polemic which it develops (symbolically and indirectly) for an ideology of poetry—for its assumed concepts of imagination, creative power, and the value of cultural reconciliations—draws its importance not from the Truth-content of the ideas but from the human commitment with which they have been invested. "Kubla Khan" is important as poetry not because it is an oblique presentation of certain abstract ideas, and not because it is a symbolic presentation of certain non-rational beliefs; it is important as a direct representation, in emotional terms, of the human conflicts which are necessarily involved in their relations. The poem draws its authority from the weight of its belief in itself, which includes the willingness to face and to bear the consequences which are entailed in its commitments.

Some of these consequences are apparent enough from "Kubla Khan" itself, whose concepts of poetic creation and cultural mastership are, as we have seen, troubled and problematic. Some of the consequences would not be elaborated, however, until later circumstances made a critical view of the poem a possibility. In fact, such a view began to develop in Coleridge's lifetime, among the later Romantics, and it even made a few bold invasions into Coleridge's own work.

Early in his life Coleridge called the masters of culture "poets," but later they became what he called "the clerisy," that more widely distributed network of individuals and social institutions which we now call "ideological state apparatuses."[8] The shift in Coleridge's emphasis reveals two important matters about his intellectual beliefs. First, Coleridge never ceased to believe that ideas shaped historical events—that thought always preceded and determined action rather than the other way round. Second, even as Coleridge (like Hegel) saw real human history flow unselfconsciously out of the precedent Idea, he lost his conviction that this pattern could be surely grasped, even unselfconsciously, in the single inspired individual. The macrocosm was firmly fixed in the realm of transcendent Ideas, and its historical continuance could be counted on through the institutional forms. The more fundamental idea, however, of the determining primacy of the creative person, collapsed under the pressures which Coleridge's own mental pursuits placed upon it.

This situation is what makes a work like "Constancy to an Ideal Object" so important in Coleridge's poetic corpus. The poem opens dramatically, with Coleridge beset by an abstract malaise:

> Since all that beat about in Nature's range,
> Or veer or vanish; why should'st thou remain
> The only constant in a world of change,
> O yearning Thought! that liv'st but in the brain?
> (1-4)

Nothing seems dependable or secure around him, but what is most troubling, for Coleridge and for the reader, is Coleridge's inability to find any consolation in the "constancy" of his "yearning thought." In the end Coleridge presents this ideal constancy—this life defended against its vicissitudes by the firmness of its ideal attachments—as the ignorant pursuit of an illusion, even a potential disaster.

> And art thou nothing? Such thou art, as when
> The woodman winding westward up the glen
> At wintry dawn, where o'er the sheep-track's maze
> The viewless snow-mist weaves a glist'ning haze,
> Sees full before him, gliding without tread,
> An image with a glory round its head;
> The enamoured rustic worships its fair hues,
> Nor knows he makes the shadow, he pursues!
> (25-32)

The pursuit of such illusions, called Brocken spectres in German, occurs throughout the literature of the period, and it is a pursuit fraught with peril. In an English context one perhaps recalls most vividly George Colwan's sinister encounter with the apparition of his brother at the top of Arthur's Seat in Hogg's *Private Memoirs and Confessions of a Justified Sinner* (1824).[9] Here in Coleridge's poem the threat is raised against the spiritual and intellectual life only.

Once again the theme of loss appears dominant in Coleridge's verse, but now what seems in greatest danger is individual identity itself. Coleridge's constancy to his ideal object has thrust him into a hall of mirrors where personality, thought, and the objects of one's love and attention all begin to lose themselves in a strange series of reflections and displacements.

> Yet still thou haunt'st me; and though well I see,
> She is not thou, and only thou art she,
> Still, still as though some dear embodied Good,
> Some living Love before my eyes there stood
> With answering look a ready ear to lend,
> I mourn to thee and say—'Ah! loveliest friend!
> That this the meed of all my toils might be,
> To have a home, an English home, and thee!'
> Vain repetition! Home and Thou are one.
> The peacefull'st cot, the moon shall shine upon,
> Lulled by the thrush and wakened by the lark,
> Without thee were but a becalmed bark,
> Whose Helmsman on an ocean waste and wide
> Sits mute and pale his mouldering helm beside.
>   (11-24)

The poem never provides a distinct referent for the feminine pronoun, though "she" seems most closely associated with the loved object of the "yearning thought." But the ambiguous use of pronouns, and the equally ambiguous syntaxes, prevent any certainty: the object of direct address in lines 16-18 seems at once the yearning thought ("thee") and the loved object ("she"), but even that identity is not certain. The final eight lines appear to be addressed to the "Thought," but because the entire poem is located in psychic space, the pronominal references are always liable to a process of transformation. "Thou" in line 25 can just as easily be read as the "Coleridge" who is undergoing his own self-interrogation.

The poem finally passes a most devastating judgment upon Coleridge's cherished belief that the realm of ideas provides a ground for reality. A constancy to an ideal object ends not so much in an inconstancy such as one finds "in Nature's range"; it finishes in a permanence more fearful than all the veils of Maya. Elsewhere Coleridge named it "Limbo," a state of "positive negation" rather than perfect emptiness: an aggressive condition of vacancy where recognized identities undergo a process of dissolution, disappearance, and fragmentation. Coleridge—as it were the fool persisting in the folly of his own convictions—arrives at a terrible wisdom in poems of this kind. Here the forms of worship implicit in such great poetic tales as "Kubla Khan" are removed from their original (symbolic) medium and immersed in a critical solution of allegory. The consequence is a new kind of poetic tale whose function is purely critical and disillusioning.

10

Phases of English Romanticism

The despair which characterizes works of this sort should not be read as a mark of artistic weakness. Of course, "Constancy to an Ideal Object" is a "secondary" work in Coleridge's corpus, in two senses: first, its tactics and purposes are defined in terms of precedent and therefore "primary" works like "Kubla Khan"; second, its self-critical relations within the Coleridge canon do not permit it an avenue for making or even anticipating new ideological affirmations. The significance of a book like *Lyrical Ballads* lies in its ability to look before and after. The critique developed in that volume is directed toward precedent ideological structures, but it is a critique whose function is to open up new ways of thinking and feeling about the human world. It too is a "secondary" work, then, as are all human works, but its secondariness is not in the field of its own purposes. Self-criticism in *Lyrical Ballads* is subordinated to the adventure of exploring the limits of a new ideological program.

Differences of these kinds remind us that the Romantic Period is marked throughout by various sorts of important differentials, and that current academic interest in the uniformities of Romanticism have tended to obscure both the fact as well as the significance of such differentials. For instance, not all of the writers of this period are Romantic writers, nor are all of the most important writers or works "Romantic" in style or ideological focus. Critics do not mark out such differentials often enough, and the failure to do so produces serious scholarly distortions of various kinds. Indeed, the differences between the first and the second generation of English Romantics is too often glanced over, and the result has been a somewhat distorted critical view of the Romantic Movement largely considered. This distortion is in fact a function of present ideological commitments, so that any scholarly effort to rectify the distortion must have as much critical impact upon the present as it does upon the past. At this point, then, I should like to introduce some comments upon the different "phases" of the English Romantic Movement. I hope it will be apparent, from the commentary itself, that these remarks involve a critical analysis of Romantic Ideology both in its early nineteenth century formations as well as in its later (literary critical) transformations as we can observe them in our own period and institutions.

Perhaps the best examples of "primary" Romantic works, in the sense I have put forward above, are to be found in the early Blake: in the *Songs*, for example, or *The Marriage of Heaven and Hell*. Works like these possess an unusual confidence in the mutually constructive powers of imagination and criticism when both operate dialectically. *The Marriage of Heaven and Hell*, for example, institutes a broad critique of inherited religion, philosophy, artistic production, and society. Its breadth appears most clearly in the poem's attack upon Swedenborgianism and the New Jerusalem Church, under whose tutelage Blake learned his own powers of criticism and first gained his imaginative freedom. Yet the critique acquires its authority not because it brings every aspect of Blake's social world within its purview, but because it is carried out in a spirit of exuberance and sympathetic imaginative understanding. The unregenerate angel, the starry kings of this world, the crippled gods of the Jewish and Christian dispensations are all brought, like errant children, within the embrace of Blake's benevolent Satanism. Blake chooses to tell poetic tales out of the history of human forms of worship, and generosity comes to replace prohibition as the medium and ground of criticism.

Works of this kind—they are rare in the period—I would call "primary" because they do not bring their own dialectical stance into question. They possess the special historical privilege which attaches to English Romantic poems written before the Reign of Terror, the Directory, and Napoleon's accession to power, as well as the political events in England which took place in response to continental circumstances. Unlike *The Marriage of Heaven and Hell*, the poems in *Lyrical Ballads* are already self-troubled by their own critical structures, and hence already anticipate (or even manifest) the "secondary" forms which will appear in "Peele Castle" or "Constancy to an Ideal Object." Byron first defines the second generation of English Romanticism, in *Childe Harold's Pilgrimage* (1812), with a work which takes its initial stance in a "secondary" posture of Romantic despair and cynicism. Harold Bloom's theory of poetic belatedness seems to me an historical myth designed to explain this fact about most of the important Romantic works: that they are typically reactionary—revisionist, "secondary," and self-critical.

In studying English Romanticism, then, we must be prepared to distinguish three different phases, as it were, of "primary" (visionary) and "secondary" (or revisionist) relationships. In Blake, *The Marriage of Heaven and Hell* is "primary" in relation to works like *Milton* and *Jerusalem*, which are "secondary" and revisionist in this structure of relations. The period covered here stretches from 1789 to approximately 1807-8, or the years between the beginning of the French Revolution to the start of the Peninsular War. In Wordsworth and Coleridge, on the other hand, we can observe a second phase of Romantic relationships. Here the initial works date from the Reign of Terror and they first appear in *Lyrical Ballads*. These works differ from Blake's in that they are already laden with self-critical and revisonist elements. Wordsworth's purely "secondary" phase is brief to the point of non-existence, for his greatest works—which are rightly judged the touchstone of first generation English Romantic poetry—incorporate vision and its critique from the start. The general historical limits to his important work—approximately 1797 to 1807—help to elucidate the differences which separate Wordsworth from Blake. Within his own corpus, "Peele Castle" is about as close as we come to a genuinely "secondary" work by Wordsworth, though even here the term is not neatly applicable since "Peele Castle" and "Tintern Abbey" are only separated from each other, ideologically and stylistically, by a difference in emphasis. The fact seems to be, as Bloom has observed, that

Wordsworth's greatest poems are all marked by a sense of belatedness.

This characteristic of Wordsworth's poetry renders Coleridge's career, from the point of view of literary criticism, all the more significant. The notorious waning of Wordsworth's poetic powers after 1807 signals what for him amounts to a "secondary" poetic phase. In Coleridge, however, the utter despair that might have been Wordsworth's late or "secondary" subject emerges clearly and forcibly in poems like "Limbo," "Constancy to an Ideal Object," "Nature," and "Love's Apparition and Evanishment." These are among the works which stand in a secondary or critical relation to works like "Kubla Khan" and "The Rime of the Ancient Mariner." The despair of such later poetry is the sign of its ideological truthfulness. Since Coleridge's great early poetry is clearly "secondary" and self-critical in its focus, however, we have to approach his later poems in terms of the ideological climate which we associate with the generation of the so-called "Younger Romantics," who occupy a third phase of the English Romantic Movement.

This third phase of Romantic relationships appears most typically in the period stretching from approximately 1808 to 1824—the literary years of a Romanticism in England which is initiated, dominated, and closed by Byron. In its primary phase Byron's work is already so deeply self-critical and revisionist that its ideology—in contrast to Blake, Wordsworth, and the early Coleridge—has to be defined in negative terms: nihilism, cynicism, anarchism. Byron woke to find himself made famous by his despair, even as England's struggle with the purposeless force of Napoleonism was to culminate in the pyrrhic victory of Waterloo, which established the ground for the Holy Alliance and the ghostly return of pre-revolutionary political structures throughout Europe. It is no mere coincidence that Byron, Shelley, and Keats all die out of England, or that Byron's and Shelley's poetry ultimately rests in an expatriate stance. The work of all three is produced in a remarkable span of English history marked, on the one hand, by domestic and foreign events of the greatest moment and, on the other, by the manifest absence of a moral or spiritual focus. Human events seemed dominated by what Shelley called the selfish and calculating principle: at home, the Regency; in the international sphere, Metternich, Castlereagh, and the Quadruple Alliance. Byron's

departure from England in 1816 is normally thought of in relation to his marriage separation, but that domestic event merely
culminated his desperate Years of Fame, which at the time he
characterized in the following epigram.

> 'Tis said Indifference marks the present time,
> Then hear the reason—though 'tis told in rhyme—
> A king who *can't*, a Prince of Wales who *don't*,
> Patriots who *sha'n't*, and Ministers who *won't*,
> What matters who are in or out of place,
> The *Mad*, the *Bad*, the *Useless*, or the *Base*?

The mordant wit of these lines would resonate, in later years,
through international events of an even more dispiriting kind.
Byron entered into the Carbonari movement and the Greek
struggle with a will, it is true, but with few illusions.

> When a man hath no freedom to fight for at home,
>   Let him combat for that of his neighbours;
> Let him think of the glories of Greece and of Rome,
>   And get knock'd on the head for his labours.
> To do good to mankind is the chivalrous plan,
>   And is always as nobly requited;
> Then battle for freedom wherever you can,
>   And, if not shot or hang'd, you'll get knighted.[12]

The greatest poetry of the later English Romantics, that is to
say, was written in a period of intense (and largely successful)
Reaction. What made the period especially debilitating to their
moral sensibilities was the fact that no one who lived through it
was able to say—as Wordsworth once and truly said—that they
had known a dawn in whose light it had been bliss to be alive.
The French Revolution was no more than a betrayed memory
for the later Romantics, the spirit of whose age was very
different from the one in which Blake, Wordsworth, and
Coleridge produced their most significant work. One of the most
profoundly optimistic spirits who ever wrote English poetry,
Shelley himself only preserved his human commitments by cast-
ing his work into a future tense: a prophetic poetry born, like
Isaiah's, in exile and captivity, and not, like Virgil's, in the com-
forts of Imperial favor. These are the circumstances which give

an edge of bleakness even to Shelley's most splendid revolutionary work, and which justify Richard Holmes's summary of
Prometheus Unbound.

> Prometheus represents suffering, hope, creative skill and
> the eternal struggle for a potential freedom. He is the
> symbol of those who struggle for the future; he is the
> symbol of those who wait the revolution, the new gol-
> den age; but he cannot be the symbol of Victory itself.[13]

Unlike Byron, Shelley never believed that it might be possible to make a moral or poetic virtue out of his despair (although
this is precisely what Shelley finally did). Nevertheless, we will
not feel the meaning or appreciate the significance of his famous
ideology of hope if we do not see how deeply it is allied to his
sense of hopelessness. The sonnet "England in 1819" expresses
this relation with great economy.

> An old, mad, blind, despised, and dying king;
> Princes, the dregs of their dull race, who flow
> Through public scorn,—mud from a muddy spring;
> Rulers who neither see, nor feel, nor know,
> But leechlike to their fainting country cling,
> Till they drop, blind in blood, without a blow.
> A people starved and stabbed in the untilled field;
> An army, whom liberticide and prey
> Makes as a two-edged sword to all who wield;
> Golden and sanguine laws which tempt and slay;
> Religion Christless, Godless—a book sealed;
> A Senate, Time's worst statute, unrepealed,
> Are graves from which a glorious Phantom may
> Burst, to illumine our tempestuous day.[14]

Nothing could be more exquisitely Shelleyan than that sly, sad
pun on the word "sanguine." At the same time, nothing could be
more telling than the subjunctive note on which the poem concludes. The sonnet is constructed out of a dreadful list of
present-tense realities. What it hopes for, however, is not even a
future in which these shall be no more. The poem is more modest and far sadder than that. It hopes for just a future promise, a
glimpse of some far goal in time. Here Shelley looks to the possibility that the evils of his day will be at least revealed, that an

age dominated by "golden and sanguine laws" will be unmasked and seen for what it is. Such knowledge "may" come, and if it were to come a new day might then be a possibility.

This is the consciousness out of which Shelley's greatest works were created. He was moved by the revolution in Spain, by the Carbonari, and especially by the Greek struggle for independence. But his enthusiasm was guarded with fear and suspicion, not least of all toward himself.

> And public attention is now centred on the wonderful revolution in Greece. I dare not, after the events of last winter, hope that slaves can become freemen so cheaply; yet I know one Greek of the highest qualities, both of courage and conduct, the Prince Mavrocordato.[15]

This was written in September 1821. Two weeks before his death his tone had changed, but only for the worse. He returned to his favorite images of blood and gold to characterize the times.

> The destiny of man can scarcely be so degraded that he was born only to die: and if such should be the case, delusions, especially the gross and preposterous ones of the existing religion, can scarcely be supposed to exalt it;—if every man said what he thought, it could not subsist a day. But all, more or less, subdue themselves to the element that surrounds them, and contribute to the evils they lament by the hypocrisy that springs from them.—England appears to be in a desperate condition, Ireland still worse, and no class of those who subsist on the public labour will be persuaded that *their* claims on it must be diminished. But the government must content itself with less in taxes, the landholder must submit to receive less rent, and the fundholder a diminished interest,—or they will all get nothing, or something worse [than] nothing.—I am glad that my good genius said *refrain*. I see little public virtue, and I foresee that the contest will be one of blood and gold two elements, which however much to my taste in my pockets and my veins, I have an objection to out of them.[16]

The special quality of Shelley's skepticism is a function of certain public and private circumstances, on the one hand, and certain ideological commitments on the other. His belief that

poets were the unacknowledged legislators of the world—the
emphasis must be placed on "unacknowledged" to specify the
Romanticism of the idea—was one shared by all the Romantics,
late and early alike. The poet's privilege was insight and
vision, the power to apprehend fundamental truths which cus-
tom and habit kept hidden from the ordinary person's consciousness. In the early Romantics, the circumstantial threats
raised against this conviction not only produced their greatest
poetry, it forced them to the most profound defenses and expli-
cations of their ideas (the Preface to *Lyrical Ballads*, the "Vision
of the Last Judgement," the *Biographia Literaria*). In each case
the ideology of poetic vision took its stand in acts of poetic displacement which were able to produce an immediate poetic contact (an aesthesis) with the Idea and "the life of things." We have
already observed this effect in a poem like "Kubla Khan"; Blake
and Wordsworth exhibit or define its contours at least as clearly,
and far more often.

> Imagination—here the Power so called
> Through sad incompetence of human speech,
> That awful Power rose from the mind's abyss
> Like an unfathered vapour that enwraps,
> At once, some lonely traveller. I was lost;
> Halted without an effort to break through;
> But to my conscious soul I now can say—
> 'I recognise thy glory:' in such strength
> Of usurpation, when the light of sense
> Goes out, but with a flash that has revealed
> The invisible world, doth greatness make abode.
> (*Prelude* VI, 592-602)

And I know that This World is a World of Imagination
& Vision. I see Every thing I paint In This World, but
Every body does not see alike. To the Eyes of a Miser a
Guinea is far more beautiful than the Sun, & a bag
worn with the use of Money has more beautiful proportions than a Vine filled with Grapes. The tree which
moves some to tears of joy is in the Eyes of others only
a Green thing which stands in the way. Some see Nature
all Ridicule & Deformity, & by these I shall not regulate
my proportions; & some scarce see Nature at all. But to

the Eyes of the Man of Imagination, Nature is Imagination itself. As a man is, so he sees. As the Eye is
formed, such are its Powers. You certainly Mistake,
when you say that the Visions of Fancy are not to be
found in This World. To Me This World is all One continued Vision of Fancy or Imagination. (Letter to
Trusler, 23 Aug. 1799)[17]

When we turn to the later Romantics the differences appear
in character rather than in kind, though they are none the less
clear for that. All the positions taken up by the early Romantics
assume more extreme forms in the later Romantics. The power
of imagination to effect an unmediated (that is, an aesthetic)
contact with noumenal levels of reality—the ideology of such a
conviction—shifts toward a naked and powerful sensationalism
in the later Romantics—an aesthetic of arresting surface effects,
a physique of poetry. Shelley's overwhelming verse effects—one
recalls especially Act II scene 5 of *Prometheus Unbound*, or the
concluding stanzas of *Adonais*, or various passages in
"Epipsychidion"—illustrate his version of this new poetic mode
very well.

> We shall become the same, we shall be one
> Spirit within two frames, oh! wherefore two?
> One passion in twin-hearts, which grows and grew,
> Till like two meteors of expanding flame,
> Those spheres instinct with it become the same,
> Touch, mingle, are transfigured; ever still
> Burning, yet ever inconsumable:
> In one another's substance finding food,
> Like flames too pure and light and unimbued
> To nourish their bright lives with baser prey,
> Which point to Heaven and cannot pass away:
> One hope within two wills, one will beneath
> Two overshadowing minds, one life, one death,
> One Heaven, one Hell, one immortality
> And one annihilation.
>
> ("Epipsychidion" 573-87)

One could cite analogous examples out of Byron's kaleidoscope
or Keats's voluptuousness, but two of their brief prose remarks
are perhaps even more telling:

the great object of life is Sensation—to feel that we exist—even though in pain. (Letter to Annabelle Milbanke, 6 Sept. 1813)

O for a Life of Sensations rather than of Thoughts!
(Letter to Bailey, 22 Nov. 1817)[18]

From the earliest commentators, like Hazlitt and Hallam, to the most recent, readers have always remarked on this difference between Byron, Shelley, and Keats on the one hand, and Wordsworth and Coleridge on the other, and many have used the difference to set (or insinuate) comparative valuations, usually to the detriment of the later Romantics. Such differences have to do with poetic style and ideology, however, not with the relative success in the poetic craft. Indeed, I do not see how the later Romantics could have written poetry at all without finding an appropriate stylistic means for revealing the special human truths of their worlds—a poetry capable of reciprocating the forms of life and behavior peculiar to the period which extends from the opening of the Peninsular War to Byron's death just prior to the close of the Greek struggle for independence.

These special circumstances affected the earlier Romantics as well. Blake fell silent, Wordsworth fell asleep, and Coleridge fell into his late Christian *contemptus*. The second generation Romantics, however, fashioned from these evil times a new set of poetic opportunities. Three sorts of poetry may be particularly noted, and although each is most closely associated with one of the three late Romantics, the three modes appear in one form or another, at one time or another, in all of these poets, and even occasionally in the early Romantics. The descriptive terms I am using here to set forth these distinctions are appropriated from the language of critics who have been largely hostile toward the work of the later Romantics.

The tradition which has attacked Byron for his sensationalism and his high-energy rhetoric is well established and has some important subsidiary strains (Byron's anti-intellectualism, his lack of thought, and so forth). Shelley, on the other hand, has always suffered from critics who deplore, or pity, his social commitments and hopes. Shelley is a cureless idealist—a meliorist, a futurist, an escapist with a vaporous style to match his airy thoughts and dreams. Keats, finally, develops his own special forms of escapism which have commonly been ranged under the general heading of his aestheticism. Let me re-emphasize here what I have alrady suggested several times. Although these characterizations bear negative judgments with which I do not agree, they also manipulate what seem to me quite shrewd and accurate critical responses. Shelley's idealism, Byron's sensationalism, and Keats's aesthetic poetry are all displaced yet fundamental vehicles of cultural analysis and critique: a poetry of extremity and escapism which is the reflex of the circumstances in which their work, their lives, and their culture were all forced to develop.

Before looking briefly at each of these poets in turn, let me recall for a moment the eroticism which is a marked feature of all their work. Of the earlier Romantics only Blake took up erotic subjects with a comparable directness, and his work differs from that of the later Romantics in being analytic and critical where they are voluptuous and sensational. This erotic strain in the verse of Byron, Shelley, and Keats has been variously deplored, condescended to, and set aside by a great many critics, particularly on the grounds that such work lacks the highest sort of artistic seriousness. But Shelley's comments on the erotic poetry of the Hellenistic and late Roman periods offers a much finer basis for a critical assessment:

> It is not what the erotic writers have, but what they have not, in which their imperfection consists. It is not inasmuch as they were Poets, but inasmuch as they were not Poets, that they can be considered with any plausibility as connected with the corruption of their age. Had that corruption availed so as to extinguish in them the sensibility to pleasure, passion, and natural scenery, which is imputed to them as an imperfection, the last triumph of evil would have been achieved. For the end of social corruption is to destroy all sensibility to pleasure; and, therefore, it is corruption. It begins at the imagination and the intellect as at the core, and distributes itself thence as a paralysing venom, through the affections into the very appetites, until all become a torpid mass in which sense hardly survives. At the approach of such a period, Poetry ever addresses itself to those faculties which are the last to be destroyed, and its voice is heard, like the footsteps of Astraea, departing from the world.[19]

What Shelley observes here is peculiarly apposite to certain aspects of his own period, as he was well aware. His remarks serve to highlight the critical function of such poetry, especially as it operates in decadent and morally imperialist cultures, or as it is judged by sensibilities which maintain and defend the ideologies of those cultures. Eroticism, Shelley argues, is the imagination's last line of human resistance against what he elsewhere called "Anarchy": political despotism and moral righteousness on the one hand, and on the other selfishness, calculation, and social indifference.

11

Shelley's Poetry:

The Judgment of the Future

We may well begin with Shelley, in fact, for his mind is the most intellectually probing of all the later Romantics. From "Alastor" (1816) to the uncompleted "The Triumph of Life" (1822) Shelley's work is marked by a poetic commitment to social melioration and by a reciprocal sense that circumstances seemed forever conspiring against such commitments. Of course, as Shelley was well aware, it was the manipulation of circumstances by certain institutions and their masters which produced both this appearance and this result. His pattern of thought crystalizes in a letter to Peacock of March 1820, written just after Shelley had news of the Cato Street Conspiracy.

> I see with deep regret in today's Papers the attempt to assassinate the Ministry. Every thing seems to conspire against Reform.— How Cobbett must laugh at the 'resumption of gold payments.' I long to see him. I have a motto on a ring in Italian—'Il buon tempo verra.'— There is a tide both in public & in private affairs, which awaits both men & nations.[20]

The motto on that ring, which Shelley wore for the rest of his life, must be seen as the sign under which his poetry was written. It is the motto of the "sages" he speaks of in *Epipsychidion*, those

> to whom this world of life
> Is as a garden ravaged, and whose strife
> Tills for the promise of a later birth
> The wilderness of this Elysian earth. (186-9)

These lines are perfectly congruent with the polemic in *A Philosophic View of Reform*, with the aesthetic of *A Defense of Poetry*, and with the famous "Preface" to *Prometheus Unbound* where Shelley sets a futurist stamp upon his poetic work.

> My purpose has hitherto been simply to familiarize the highly refined imagination of the more select classes of poetical readers with beautiful idealisms of moral excellence; aware that until the mind can love, and admire, and trust, and hope, and endure, reasoned principles of moral conduct are seeds cast upon the highway of life which the unconscious passenger tramples into dust, although they would bear the harvest of his happiness.

In the verse itself, this future-oriented program is equally unmistakable. The cave to which Prometheus and Asia retire at the end of Act III is a source and a womb, a place from which the renovated future will one day spring (as it has sprung recurrently in the past) out of the fulness—and the full understanding—of history. Its present tense is fashioned in a mode of preserving, nurturing, feeding, and growing. In "Epipsychidion" it is represented thus:

> I have sent books and music there, and all
> Those instruments with which high Spirits call
> The future from its cradle, and the past
> Out of its grave, and make the present last
> In thoughts and joys which sleep, but cannot die.
> (519-23)

In *Prometheus Unbound* this present tense of effort and expecta-
tion and desire succeeds to the futurist vision of Act III Scene 4
where the Spirit of the Hour, dispatched to observe the New
Day in Scene 3, returns to the cave to tell Prometheus and Asia
of what he has seen. His report (lines 98ff.) is an angelic (but
not, as we shall see, an ineffectual) dream:

> And behold, thrones were kingless, and men walked
> One with the other even as spirits do,
> None fawned, none trampled; hate, disdain, or fear,
> Self-love or self-contempt, on human brows
> No more inscribed, as o'er the gate of hell,
> 'All hope abandon ye who enter here;'
> None frowned, none trembled, none with eager fear
> Gazed on another's eye of cold command,
> Until the subject of a tyrant's will
> Became worse fate, the abject of his own,
> Which spurred him, like an outspent horse, to death.
> None wrought his lips in truth-entangling lines
> Which smiled the lie his tongue disdained to speak;
> None, with firm sneer, trod out in his own heart
> The Sparks of love and hope till there remained
> Those bitter ashes, a soul self-consumed,
> And the wretch crept a vampire among men,
> Infecting all with his own hideous ill;
> None talked that common, false, cold, hollow talk
> Which makes the heart deny the *yes* it breathes,
> Yet question that unmeant hypocrisy
> With such a self-mistrust as has no name.
> And women too, frank, beautiful, and kind
> As the free heaven which rains fresh light and dew
> On the wide earth, past; gentle radiant forms,
> From custom's evil taint exempt and pure;
> Speaking the wisdom once they could not think,
> Looking emotions once they feared to feel,
> And changed to all which once they dared not be,
> Yet being now, made earth like heaven;
>
> (*Prometheus Unbound* III, 4, 131-60)

This is not an instance of Shelley's greatest poetry, but it is a
useful passage for that very reason. It contains a statement of his

liberal and reformist ideology, an advanced (and therefore still attractive) set of ideas for his period, but almost pure ideology nonetheless. Time does not treat such verse very kindly. Poetry's first obligation is to reveal the contradictory forces which human beings at once generate and live through, and its second is to provide the reader, both contemporary and future alike, with the basis for a sympathetic and critical assessment of those forces. This passage from *Prometheus Unbound* does not perform either of those functions especially well.

We may contrast it, therefore, with the great conclusion to *Adonais*:

52

The One remains, the many change and pass;
Heaven's light forever shines, Earth's shadows fly;
Life, like a dome of many-coloured glass,
Stains the white radiance of Eternity
Until Death tramples it to fragments.—Die,
If thou wouldst be with that which thou dost seek!
Follow where all is fled!—Rome's azure sky,
Flowers, ruins, statues, music, words, are weak
The glory they transfuse with fitting truth to speak.

53

Why linger, why turn back, why shrink, my Heart?
Thy hopes are gone before: from all things here
They have departed; thou shouldst now depart!
A light is passed from the revolving year,
And man, and woman; and what still is dear
Attracts to crush, repels to make thee wither.
The soft sky smiles,—the low wind whispers near:
'Tis Adonais calls! oh, hasten thither,
No more let Life divide what Death can join together.

The stunning rhetorical question that opens stanza 53 provides a convenient focus for what is most central to this poetry. On the one hand it introduces the later imperative ("oh, hasten thither"), but on the other it exposes the pathos and sense of loss which is involved in Shelley's assault on death and the future. The present is an evil time, a place of corruption, but if it "stains the white radiance of Eternity"—if Shelley unequivocally exposes its evil—he also cannot let his poetry betray any aspect of the human world. So he compares life's "stain" to the decorative parti-colored panes which fragment the sunlight streaming through the "dome of many-coloured glass." These sorts of alternating and contradictory sympathies in the poetry help to explain why his heart lingers, shrinks, and wants to turn back even as it pursues the call of Adonais:

54

That Light whose smile kindles the Universe,
That beauty in which all things work and move,
That Benediction which the eclipsing Curse
Of birth can quench not, that sustaining Love
Which through the web of being blindly wove
By man and beast and earth and air and sea,
Burns bright or dim, as each are mirrors of
The fire for which all thirst; now beams on me,
Consuming the last clouds of cold mortality.

55

The breath whose might I have invoked in song
Descends on me; my spirit's bark is driven,
Far from the shore, far from the trembling throng
Whose sails were never to the tempest given;
The massy earth and sphered skies are riven!
I am borne darkly, fearfully, afar;
Whilst, burning through the inmost veil of Heaven,
The soul of Adonais, like a star,
Beacons from the abode where the Eternal are.

Shelley's poem is itself a portion of the dome of many-coloured glass. In the end he bequeaths it to the future, which is imaged, for him, as the "abode" and afterlife inhabited by Adonais (the place or time where Adonais will at last be recognized as a "star"). But Shelley's verse never for a moment allows us to forget that his implacable futurism is a function of his present attachments—indeed, is a displaced reflection of his immediate (frustrated) "hopes." What moves us in Shelley's poetry is his devotion to the realities of the human world he knows, and ultimately to the Idea of a fully human world. That devotion appears most graphically when it is represented in all its adversative conditions, and most particularly in its own contradictions. These are inherent in the image of a voyage from "cold mortality" to the "abode where the Eternal are," and they appear as the emotional contradictions which accompany the production of the poetic images.

From the subsequent reader's point of view, however, this poetry must not be turned into a destructive form of worship, the locus of a sentimental idea which would support an ideology or displacement. Shelley's poetic achievement is allied to the project of Blake's Los: both aim to keep the poetic vision in a time of trouble (*Jerusalem* 30:15). Later readers must recognize such a project for what it is, must submit it to an historical analysis in order to establish its special human limits. Such an analysis helps to distinguish the ideological, the stylistic, and the emotional aspects of poetic work, and thereby to reveal the network of relations which subsist between them in particular poems. Shelley's ideology is time and place specific. His poems incorporate that ideology and thereby specify and generate the stylistic tensions and emotional contradictions which appear in the work. Shelley's futurism is not a model for human life, then, it is an example of a human life. In its perfect articulation lies a critical challenge.

12

Byron's Ideal of Immediacy

Shelley's futurist orientation is allied to Keats's aestheticism, where the contradictions of an escape into poetry—the impulse to attempt such an escape as well as the impasse which it must thereby create and reveal—are everywhere brilliantly dramatized. Arnold recognized this quality in Keats's verse but, for reasons very much his own, he was unable to appreciate its full critical significance. Since I have discussed these matters at length elsewhere,[21] I want to turn to another and perhaps even closer ally of Shelley's, to Byron. Both occupied the ideological vanguard of their period and both actively engaged in progressive social action at political and ideological levels. Consequently, some critics have been reluctant to associate their work with "escapist" moves and tendencies, which seem to them critical characterizations that betray or ignore the poets' activist commitments. I wish to argue here, however, that Byron and Shelley are most deeply *engaged* (in a socialist-activist sense) when they have moved furthest along their paths of displacement and escape. This aspect of their work is what allies them to the "Romanticism" of all the other Romantic poets, from the most reactionary, like Coleridge, to the most aesthetic, like Keats. More than this, the displacements of Shelley and Byron provide their work with its critical and cutting edge. In Shelley's contradictory futurism lies a fearful judgment upon what men were making of other men in Shelley's world. Byron's despair—both in its comic and in its violent modes—must be seen in the same way.

We may begin our survey of Byron with a final glance at Shelley, and particularly at Shelley's enthusiasm for the Greek Revolution. On this topic one of Shelley's greatest critics, Kenneth Neill Cameron, has written:

> The most encouraging and significant event on the continent, Shelley felt, was the beginning, in 1821, of the revolutionary war of the Greek people, significant because it represented the first major cracking of the Metternich system, and hence a culminating point in the historical evolution of the forces of liberty. It is in this perspective that he treats the Greek revolution in "Hellas" putting into flaming lyrical verse the same concept of historical development we have already noted in his prose.[22]

But *Hellas*—that "classic English statement of Philhellenism," as Richard Holmes has rightly said—is, like *Prometheus Unbound*, "almost entirely visionary and mystic"[23] in its formulation. Furthermore, although Cameron represents the Greek revolution as a significant crack in the structure of the Holy Alliance, it was far from being that. Rather, it represented the beginning of the end of the Turkish Empire and the definitive emergence of European imperialism—at the head of which was England—into world history. Shelley's philhellenism, like Byron's, was a nostalgic attachment to their image of a human civilization.

> We are all Greeks. Our laws, our literature, our religion, our arts have their root in Greece. But for Greece—Rome, the instructor, the conqueror, or the metropolis of our ancestors, would have spread no illumination with her arms, and we might still have been savages and idolaters; or, what is worse, might have arrived at such a stagnant and miserable state of social institution as China and Japan possess. The human form and the human mind attained to a perfection in Greece which has impressed its image on those faultless productions, whose very fragments are the despair of modern art, and has propagated impulses which cannot cease, through a thousand channels of manifest or imperceptible operation, to ennoble and delight mankind until the extinction of the race.[24]

These ideas are typical philhellenist illusions[25] and, as such, were open to a political exploitation by Europe's imperialist powers, as well as a poetical exploitation by writers like Shelley and Byron. In Byron, however, philhellenist idealism assumed emotional forms that were quite different from what we see in Shelley. Byron's early work, for example, generates a despair which is normally marked by a cynical recoil:

5

> Or burst the vanish'd Hero's lofty mound;
> Far on the solitary shore he sleeps:
> He fell, and falling nations mourn'd around;
> But now not one of saddening thousands weeps,
> Nor warlike-worshipper his vigil keeps
> Where demi-gods appear'd, as records tell.
> Remove yon skull from out the scatter'd heaps:
> Is that a temple where a God may dwell?
> Why ev'n the worm at last disdains her shatter'd cell!

6

Look on its broken arch, its ruin'd wall,
Its chambers desolate, and portals foul:
Yes, this was once Ambition's airy hall,
The dome of Thought, the palace of the Soul:
Behold through each lack-lustre, eyeless hole,
The gay recess of Wisdom and of Wit
And Passion's host, that never brook'd control:
Can all, saint, sage, or sophist ever writ,
People this lonely tower, this tenement refit?

7

Well didst thou speak, Athena's wisest son!
'All that we know is, nothing can be known.'
Why should we shrink from what we cannot shun?
Each has his pang, but feeble sufferers groan
With brain-born dreams of evil all their own.
Pursue what Chance or Fate proclaimeth best;
Peace waits us on the shores of Acheron:
There no forc'd banquet claims the sated guest,
But Silence spreads the couch of ever welcome rest.
(*Childe Harold* II)

In the later work the despair normally appears either as the comic pathos typified in the Haidée episode of *Don Juan,* for example, or the stoical pathos of a poem like "On This Day I Complete My Thirty-Sixth Year." In all instances, however, Greece is a poetic resort, an Ideal against which the insufficiencies of the political and cultural present can be measured and judged. Greece was Byron's most important "unreached paradise" and, therefore, the focus of his deepest despair.

Fair Greece, sad relic of departed worth!
Immortal, though no more; though fallen, great.
(*Childe Harold* II, st. 73)

A set of contradictions in itself, Byron's Greece became the catalyst which separated out whole patterns of contradictions in a world Byron spent so much of his life observing.

In this situation we can begin to see how Byron's idealisms were to become in his verse a vehicle for critical analysis. His poetry has often been an object of suspicion because it cultivates moods of despair. But as Baudelaire was the first to appreciate fully, Byron's despair, along with the entire range of his negative emotions, is the source of his greatness as a poet and his importance for the (programmatically hypocritical) reader. Byronic Despair is the reflex of an Ideal attachment in precisely the same way that Shelleyan Hope is the reflex of his Idealism. This is the structure which governs their ideological commitments. When we look at their poetical works we find that Shelley's Hope (the Ineffectual Angel) assumes various futurist modes, and that Byron's Despair (Mad Bad Lord Byron) appears in corresponding sets of sensationalist forms (in every sense). In each case the poetry develops the specific patterns of emotional and intellectual contradictions which define what is valuable in their work.

The poetical myth of his life, which Byron invented, is a convenient entrance into his works. Disheartened by his world and his own inability to alter its force or circumstance, Byron creates in his poetry a drama of the disillusioned existence. Its desperation appears in an escapist gesture of a special sort: not into the future, or into art, but into the flux of everything which is most immediate, a flight into the surfaces of poetry and life, the dance of verse, the high energy of instant sensations and feelings (whether of pleasure or pain makes no difference). In poetry this sometimes appears as the effort to break free of language altogether in order to achieve an unmediated set of responses:

108

There is the moral of all human tales;
'Tis but the same rehearsal of the past,
First Freedom, and then Glory—when that fails,
Wealth, vice, corruption,—barbarism at last.
And History, with all her volumes vast,
Hath but *one* page,—'tis better written here,
Where gorgeous Tyranny had thus amass'd
All treasures, all delights, that eye or ear,
Heart, soul could seek, tongue ask—Away with words!
                        draw near,

109

Admire, exult—despise—laugh, weep,—for here
There is such matter for all feeling:—Man!
Thou pendulum betwixt a smile and tear,
Ages and realms are crowded in this span,
This mountain, whose obliterated plan
The pyramid of empires pinnacled,
Of Glory's gewgaws shining in the van
Till the sun's rays with added flame were fill'd!
Where are its golden roofs? where those who dared to build?
                                        (*Childe Harold* IV)

At other times it appears as the effort to plunge into the verbal medium itself, to make the flow of language the encompassing totality of immediate experience. Byron's famous "spontaneity"—what Swinburne called his "sincerity and strength"—is a poetic style which covets verbal immediacy, and *Don Juan*'s digressive manner is its exemplary form. The mediations of language are destroyed by turning language into an environment for sensations and feelings. The first twelve stanzas of Canto XIV of *Don Juan* reflect upon this sort of poetic style:

7

But what's this to the purpose? you will say.
 Gent. Reader, nothing; a mere speculation,
For which my sole excuse is—'tis my way,
 Sometimes *with* and sometimes without occasion
I write what's uppermost, without delay;
 This narrative is not meant for narration,
But a mere airy and fantastic basis,
To build up common things with common places.

8

You know, or don't know, that great Bacon saith,
 "Fling up a straw, 'twill show the way the wind blows";
And such a straw, borne on by human breath,
 Is Poesy, according as the mind glows;

A paper kite, which flies 'twixt life and death,
 A shadow which the onward Soul behind throws:
And mine's a bubble not blown up for praise,
 But just to play with, as an infant plays.

. . . . .

10

I have brought this world about my ears, and eke
 The other; that's to say, the Clergy—who
Upon my head have bid their thunders break
 In pious libels by no means a few.
And yet I can't help scribbling once a week,
 Tiring old readers, nor discovering new.
In youth I wrote, because my mind was full,
And now because I feel it growing dull.

. . . .

12

I think that were I *certain* of success,
 I hardly could compose another line:
So long I've battled either more or less,
 That no defeat can drive me from the Nine.
This feeling 'tis not easy to express,
 And yet 'tis not affected, I opine.
In play, there are two pleasures for your choosing—
The one is winning, and the other losing.[26]

This hedonism of the imagination—it characterizes all three of the later Romantics, as Arthur Henry Hallam was soon to observe—is what Byron calls "The grand antithesis" to everything in his life and world which seems debased (*Don Juan* XV, st. 2). His poetic escape into immediacy is an aesthetic and critical move for "seeing matters which are out of sight" (ibid.):

Ah!—What should follow slips from my reflection:

Whatever follows ne'ertheless may be
As a propos of hope or retrospection,
As though the lurking thought had follow'd free.
All present life is but an Interjection,
An "Oh!" or "Ah!" of joy or misery,
Or a "Ha! ha!" or "Bah!"—a yawn, or "Pooh!"
Of which perhaps the latter is most true.
                    (*Don Juan* XV, st.1)

A latent cynicism and despair—the "lurking thought" behind these lines—sharpens the verse to a fine edge. Byron's attack upon the Europe of Napoleon, Metternich, and Castlereagh is made possible because he agrees in his poetry to "become what he beholds." His abandoned and sensational poetry is the reflex of the civilization which created the necessity for such a style of life and art. The poetry triumphs in its hedonism, however, whereas the objective world which it mirrors merely suffers and inflicts. The difference is a function of the reflexive (in both senses) capacity of verse. The poetry supplies a reflection of the world (as we commonly say), but the image is generated from the poetry's "reflex" or response to that world and its own act of observation. In this way the poetry draws itself into the world it is "reflecting." The process forces the poetry to become what it beholds, to translate its observations (via the images) into equivalent emotional signs, and finally to open itself to further acts of self-conscious "reflection" in (and upon) the poetry itself.

13

Romantic Illusions

and Their Contradictions

A paradox lies at the heart of Byron's sensationalism which we can begin to approach through Shelley. In his "Defense of Poetry" Shelley attacked his age for its selfishness and calculation on the one hand, and on the other for the refusal of its people to reflect upon the meaning of their forms of life:

> We have more moral, political, and historical wisdom, than we know how to reduce into practice; we have more scientific and economical knowledge than can be accommodated to the just distribution of the produce which it multiplies. The poetry in these systems of thought, is concealed by the accumulation of facts and calculating processes. . . . Our calculations have outrun conception; we have eaten more than we can digest. The cultivation of those sciences which have enlarged the limits of the empire of man over the external world, has, for want of the poetical faculty, proportionally circumscribed those of the internal world; and man, having enslaved the elements, remains himself a slave.[27]

When Shelley in another part of this passage urges his readers to imagine what they know, his plea is for an act of sympathetic and critical reflection. The fool persists in his folly to gain wisdom, and poetry is an especially useful vehicle for such a project.

The subject of Byron's poetry is the world which Shelley had in mind in the passage above. This is the environment which they, along with their contemporaries, were "doomed to inflict or bear" (*Childe Harold* III, st. 71). The grand illusion of Romantic *ideology* is that one may escape such a world through imagination and poetry. The great truth of Romantic *work* is that there is no escape, that there is only revelation (in a wholly secular sense):

> The race of life becomes a hopeless flight
> To those that walk in darkness: on the sea,
> The boldest steer but where their ports invite,
> But there are wanderers o'er Eternity
> Whose bark drives on and on, and anchored ne'er shall be.
> (*Childe Harold* III, st. 70)

What is most stirring about this great passage is the "lurking thought" of pity and despair. Imagination and poetry do not offer a relief and escape but a permanent and self-realized condition of suffering, a Romantic Agony. The "hopeless flight" of "those that walk in darkness" is not removed when that flight

131

becomes an eternal one; on the contrary, the hopelessness is raised to a pitiful and tragic level precisely because the Pilgrim of Eternity no longer has any illusions about the human world he sees, no longer has any illusions about himself. The Romantic Imagination does not save, it offers, like Keats's Moneta, a tragic understanding. And for the Romantic poet, the best and worst knowledge it brings is the critique of the ideology upon which Romantic poetry is itself founded. The judgment which it passes upon its world is therefore always justified—if it is to be justified at all—by the depth of the poetry's self-criticism. This is necessarily the case since Romantic poetry places the individual at the determining center of the human world.

Like Shelley's meliorism and Keats's aestheticism, Byron's despair is not a philosophic but an experiential datum. We are gripped by Byron's work through the medium of this despair, which becomes an ethical category only after it has first been seized as an aesthetic one. This is why Byron's poetic despair must not be a cause for our critical valuations of his poetic work: despair is not the meaning of his poetry, it is its condition of being, and the poetic reflex of the social and historical realities it is a part of.

What is true of Byron's work is true of Romantic poetry in general. It is a poetry of ideas, of Ideals, and—ultimately—of Ideology, which is why displacements and illusions are its central preoccupations and resorts. Consequently, its greatest moments of artistic success are almost always those associated with loss, failure, and defeat—in particular the losses which strike most closely to the Ideals (and Ideologies) cherished by the poets in their work.

In Keats these moments are typically related to the apparent failures of poetry and the imagination:

> Adieu! the fancy cannot cheat so well
> As she is fam'd to do, deceiving elf.
> Adieu! adieu! thy plaintive anthem fades
> Past the near meadows, over the still stream,
> Up the hill-side; and now 'tis buried deep
> In the next valley-glades:
> Was it a vision, or a waking dream?
> Fled is that music:—Do I wake or sleep?[28]

Of course, Keats's "fancy" has not failed him at all, it has simply refused to submit to the final ideological appropriation which the poem itself had proposed. The displacement efforts of Romantic poetry, its escape trails and pursued states of harmony and reconciliation—ultimately, its desire for process and endless self-reproduction ("something evermore about to be")—are that age's dominant cultural illusions which Romantic poetry assumes only to weigh them out and find them wanting.

In no poem are all these illusions exposed more terribly than in Keats's epistle commonly known as "To J. H. Reynolds, Esq.," and particularly in the great and famous passage toward the conclusion (74-105). The passage needs to be recalled in full because of its gradual movement of self-revelation. The experience of Imagination first draws Keats into a malaise of doubt (74-82), then into a positive experience of immediate dissatisfaction (82-85), and finally into a terrible vision of what, in his epoch, it would mean for something to be evermore about to be—of what is entailed in the ideology of growth and process:

> I was at home,
> And should have been most happy—but I saw
> Too far into the sea; where every maw
> The greater on the less feeds evermore:—
> But I saw too distinct into the core
> Of an eternal fierce destruction
> And so from happiness I far was gone.
> Still am I sick of it: and though to-day
> I've gathered young spring-leaves, and flowers gay
> Of periwinkle and wild strawberry,
> Still do I that most fierce destruction see,
> The shark at savage prey—the hawk at pounce,
> The gentle robin, like a pard or ounce,
> Ravening a worm.—   (92-105)

This is the displaced image from "Nature" which represents, and reflects upon, the conditions of life in the world Keats knew. Organic growth and the ideology of process are here graphically analyzed as the illusions which the cultural institutions of the age developed. These illusions attempt to disguise the horror entailed in the maintenance and reproduction of the social structures—of the human life—Keats knew, to hide from the recognition of horror.

The poetics of Romanticism supposed that in a dark time the eye might begin to see into the One Life through the Imagination, which would establish a "standard law" for the self-destructive world of one's experience. In making this supposition the poetry became what it beheld: it assumed to itself the most advanced ideology of its culture and it suffered, as a result, the contradictions of such an assumption, the meaning of the ideology. Romantic poetry pursued the illusions of its own ideas and Ideals in order to avoid facing the truths of immediate history and its own Purgatorial blind. Its triumph, and Keats's odes demonstrate this fact as well as any work produced in the period, is discovered when the pursuit is thwarted and interrupted, and finally broken.

When reading Romantic poems, then, we are to remember that their ideas—for example, ideas about the creativity of Imagination, about the centrality of the Self, about the organic and processive structure of natural and social life, and so forth—are all historically specific in a crucial and paradoxical sense. I have remarked on these matters earlier but the point is crucial and bears repeating here. In the Romantic Age these and similar ideas are represented as trans-historical—eternal truths which wake to perish never. The very belief that transcendental categories can provide a permanent ground for culture becomes, in the Romantic Age, an ideological formation—another illusion raised up to hold back an awareness of the contradictions inherent in contemporary social structures and the relations they support. As far as Romantic poetry is concerned, this General Ideology informs all its work as an implied and assumed premise which takes various forms specific to the particular writers and their circumstances.

Ideas and Ideology therefore lie at the heart of all Romantic poetry. Its entire emotional structure depends upon the credit and fidelity it gives to its own fundamental illusions. And its greatest moments usually occur when it pursues its last and final illusion: that it can expose or even that it has uncovered its illusions and false consciousness, that it has finally arrived at the Truth. The need to believe in such an achievement, either immediate or eventual, is deeply Romantic (and therefore illusive) because it locates the goal of human pursuits, needs, and desires in Ideal space. When Manfred, at the opening of his play, condemns his entire life's pursuit with the maxim "The tree of knowledge is not that of life," he lays open the heart of Romantic darkness. His manner of doing so remains, however, profoundly Romantic, as we see clearly in the drama's patterns of absolutes and ultimatums. Manfred's last cherished illusion is that he has no illusions left, that he has cleared his mind of its cant and finally knows the whole truth: "that nothing could be known" (*Don Juan* VII, st. 5).

Later scholars and readers have often absorbed the ideological commitments which these works themselves first made. A typical example of such an absorption will take the following form. The critic will trace out a pattern of "poetic development" which will show (say) Keats's or Byron's progress from certain interesting but undeveloped ideas, through various intermediate stages, to conclude in some final wisdom or "achievement."[29] In Keats criticism we recognize this as the twice-told tale of his movement from a testing and tentative commitment to the idea of the creative "fancy" to the final truths which center in ideas like "negative capability" and in poems like "To Autumn." But the fact is that Keats's aesthetic ideas were in constant flux, and they have, in any case, a purely circumstantial relation to the development of his artistic skill or the production of his artistic work. Ideas and Ideology are important for Keats's work because they help to define the concrete and specific character of different poems, and because they help to provide those poems with the terms (the images) in which their emotional dramas are played out. For Keats's poetry, the idea of negative capability is no more advanced *as an idea* than is the idea of the creative fancy. Rather, it locates a certain (as it were) psychological stage of Keats's poetic career, a special focus for the agony and strife of the human hearts he studied. Out of the advancement and the critique of this and similiar ideas Keats was able to fashion some of his greatest works; at the same time, the idea itself has been frequently debased in its critical representation. Literary criticism too often likes to transform the critical illusions of poetry into the worshipped truths of culture.

Romantic poetry presents its contradictions at the level of consciousness and as ideology, and the revelation of the contradictions takes the typical form of an immediate experience. Contradictions are *undergone* in Romantic poems, necessarily, because the ideology which informs their styles involves the supreme illusion of the trans-historical privilege of poetry and the creative imagination. This is why Romantic poets like Keats appear to suffer in and through their work, and why Keats could call a reading of *King Lear* "the fierce dispute/ Betwixt damnation and impassioned clay." The writing and the reading of poetry in a Romantic style involves the emotional experience of contradiction at the level of consciousness and in the form of Romantic ideology. This is what Shelley's famous passage on the nature of Romantic experience *means*:

> Most wretched men
> Are cradled into poetry by wrong,
> They learn in suffering what they teach in song.
> ("Julian and Maddalo," 544-6)

Shelley's presentation of the tensions and contradictions which typify Romantic poems seems preferable to the formulations of much contemporary criticism, because Shelley's verse has fewer illusions about the truths it speaks of. Famous passages like the one just quoted should remind us that in Romantic poems the tensions and contradictions appear as a drama of suffering. Furthermore, the power of such a drama has little to do with the "delight" of a happily discovered truth. On the contrary, it is either an awesome and fearful experience before which one "trembles like a guilty thing surprised," or it is the terrible knowledge of "those to whom the miseries of the world/ Are misery, and will not let them rest." Romantic poets, insofar as they are like men speaking to men, are no different from most human beings, and do not find much pleasure in having their most cherished illusions unmasked, and themselves left at the edge of defenselessness. The literary criticism of Romantic works will justify itself, therefore, when it is seen to have followed the example of the poetry itself.

14

The Critique of Poetry

and the Critique of Criticism:

An Instance from Byron

This idea that poetry, or even consciousness, can set one free of the ruins of history and culture is the grand illusion of every Romantic poet. The idea has been inherited and reproduced in the cultural support systems—principally the academy—which have followed in the wake of the Romantic Movement. In English and American culture, this idea has descended to us largely through the lines of thought which have developed out of the work of Coleridge and Hegel. As a consequence, academicians and literary commentators have turned what Blake once called "poetic tales" into "forms of worship." In current terms (or perhaps "jargon"), the ideology of Romanticism has undergone a process of cultural reification. Today the scholarship and interpretation of Romantic works is dominated by an uncritical absorption in Romanticism's own self-representations.

That my own work on Byron cannot escape the criticism of such a judgment now seems to me very clear. My interest in Byron was triggered years ago largely because he seemed so different from the other Romantics. The differences were marked out by criticism itself, which preferred to set Byron aside, or to treat his work as marginal to the central projects of Romanticism. And of course Byron is in many ways a figure who covets the stance of an "outsider", and who presented himself as "the enemy within," the gadfly and critic of his own age and culture.

Without minimizing the differential which Byron represents, I would say now that my initial enthusiasm for Byron's self-representations misled my critical judgment. The poetry of the

Romantic Movement, from its earliest to its latest transformations, is marked by extreme forms of displacement and poetic
conceptualization whereby the actual human issues with which
the poetry is concerned are resituated and deflected in various
ways. I have already described an instance of this process in
some poems by Wordsworth. I should like to conclude with an
illustrative case from Byron, partly because I have been to some
extent responsible for perpetuating certain misconceptions about
his work, and partly because Byron's late achievements can
sometimes appear to have transcended his own Romantic illusions. The "poetic development" of Byron which I argued in
Fiery Dust now seems to me a most misleading critical formulation.

Like all Romantic poetry, Byron's work is deeply self-
critical, but only as a drama in which its own illusions must be
suffered. To achieve this effect requires, therefore, that the illusions be embraced and advanced. So it is with Byron. From his
earliest to his latest work he cherished the idea (or the hope) that
he could stand above or beyond the contradictions of his age:
not merely a "grand Napoleon of the realms of rhyme" (*Don
Juan* XI, st. 55) but a superb *Citoyen du Monde* who could survey, as from "a tower upon a headlong rock" (*Childe Harold* III,
st. 41), the world of dispute and turmoil below. The grand and
pitiful illusion reached its most extreme form in *Don Juan*,
where Byron sought to establish his self-sufficiency and power
through a comic panorama of the world's folly, evil, and self-
deceptions. His last resort from his own illusions was to declare
that he was the most disillusioned of mortals—the *être suprême*
of human detachment who could at last take God's laughter
over from Milton.

The Romanticism of *Don Juan* appears as the repeated collapse of this assault upon detachment. The failures of love, the
fragility of whatever seems most to be cherished (beauty, innocence, courage, justice), the persistence of surplus evils like
indifference, cruelty, war, religion, and state power: all these
things drove Byron out of his disillusioned fastnesses and
retreats to suffer the conflict of his feelings. One immediately
recognizes such eventualities in the stories of Julia and Haidée,
in Byron's rage at his epoch's special thrones (the Church) and
principalities (the States), in his horror at the power of circumstances over human beings (the shipwreck of Canto II) and

the blind persistence of cruel practices (the Siege of Ismail). But most moving of all, perhaps, is Byron's loss of detachment in the English cantos. From Canto XI to the poem's interrupted conclusion Byron returns to the world of Regency England where his own fame was born. It is, of course, the easiest of targets for Byron, whose knowledge of that "paradise of pleasure and ennui" (*Don Juan* XIV, st. 17) was intimate and wide. So his satire unrolls itself in a splendid variety of styles which extend from the broadest ironic humor:

8

Don Juan had got out on Shooter's Hill;
 Sunset the time, the place the same declivity
Which looks along that vale of good and ill
 Where London streets ferment in full activity;
While every thing around was calm and still,
 Except the creak of wheels, which on their pivot he
Heard,—and that bee-like, bubbling, busy hum
Of cities, that boils over with their scum:—

9

I say, Don Juan, wrapt in contemplation,
 Walked on behind his carriage, o'er the summit,
And lost in wonder of so great a nation,
 Gave way to't, since he could not overcome it.
"And here," he cried, "is Freedom's chosen station;
 Here peals the people's voice, nor can entomb it
Racks, prisons, inquisitions; resurrection
Awaits it, each new meeting or election.

10

"Here are chaste wives, pure lives; here people pay
 But what they please; and if that things be dear,
'Tis only that they love to throw away
 Their cash, to show how much they have a-year.
Here laws are all inviolate; none lay

Traps for the traveller; every highway's clear;
Here"—he was interrupted by a knife,
With "Damn your eyes! your money or your life!"

to the most subtle comic revelations, such as in Canto XVI
when Juan descends to breakfast after his night encounter with
the ghost of the Black Friar:

31

She looked, and saw him pale, and turned as pale
 Herself; then hastily looked down, and muttered
Something, but what's not stated in my tale.
 Lord Henry said, his muffin was ill buttered;
The Duchess of Fitz-Fulke played with her veil,
 And looked at Juan hard, but nothing uttered.
Aurora Raby, with her large dark eyes,
Surveyed him with a kind of calm surprise.

34

Lord Henry, who had now discussed his chocolate
 Also the muffin whereof he complained,
Said, Juan had not got his usual look elate,
 At which he marvelled, since it had not rained;
Then asked her Grace what news were of the Duke of late?
 Her Grace replied, *his* Grace was rather pained
With some slight, light, hereditary twinges
Of gout, which rusts aristocratic hinges.

35

Then Henry turned to Juan and addressed
 A few words of condolence on his state:
"You look," quoth he, "as if you had had your rest
 Broke in upon by the Black Friar of late."
"What Friar?" said Juan; and he did his best
 To put the question with an air sedate,
Or careless; but the effort was not valid

To hinder him from growing still more pallid.
(*Don Juan* XVI)

In fact, however, the satire and comedy of the English cantos—so cool and so urbane—rests upon a series of contradictory emotional involvements which threaten to break through at any point, and which do so repeatedly. We observe such a moment at the outset of the English cantos, in Canto XI, where Byron's art of memory stirs up a range of complex and contradictory emotions. In stanzas 55-63, for example, when Byron surveys the recent history of English poetical fashions, his status as the world-famous expatriate bard permits him to assume an amused pose of unruffled detachment. As he begins his commentary on the literary scene of that tight little island, Byron seems all coolness and superiority.

55

In twice five years the "greatest living poet,"
 Like to the champion in the fisty ring,
Is called on to support his claim, or show it,
 Although 'tis an imaginary thing.
Even I—albeit I'm sure I did not know it,
 Nor sought of foolscap subjects to be king,—
Was reckoned, a considerable time,
The grand Napoleon of the realms of rhyme.

Ensconsed in the treasure-house of such brilliant and witty poetry, Byron can smile at his own folly from a throne of self-assurance. But as the period of his memory shifts between the present and the recent past, between 1814 and 1822, the tone also slips and shifts.

56

But Juan was my Moscow, and Faliero
 My Leipsic, and my Mount Saint Jean seems Cain:
"La Belle Alliance" of dunces down at zero,
 Now that the Lion's fall'n, may rise again:
But I will fall at least as fell my hero;
 Nor reign at all, or as a *monarch* reign;

Or to some lonely isle of Jailors go
With turncoat Southey for my turnkey Lowe.

Here the larger truth begins to emerge, that Byron is still deeply
involved, emotionally, in the pursuit of that "imaginary thing."
His comparison of this ridiculous pursuit to a pugilist's
ambition—the quest for the championship of poetry, as it
were—underscores his consciousness of the absurdity of these
things. That it is all ludicrous, even pathetic, is very clear; that
he has not given any of it over is, however, no less apparent, to
himself and us alike. Byron's poetic awareness that his own
assumed detachment is actually no more than a new form of
desired superiority drives his verse into a dazzling sequence of
stanzas whose most remarkable feature is their complex emotional shifts and contradictions.

62

This is the literary *lower* Empire,
  Where the Praetorian bands take up the matter;—
A "dreadful trade," like his who "gathers samphire,"
  The insolent soldiery to soothe and flatter,
With the same feelings as you'd coax a vampire.
  Now, were I once at home, and in good satire,
I'd try conclusions with those Janizaries,
And show them *what* an intellectual war is.

63

I think I know a trick or two, would turn
  Their flanks;—but it is hardly worth my while
With such small gear to give myself concern:
  Indeed I've not the necessary bile;
My natural temper's really aught but stern,
  And even my Muse's worst reproof's a smile;
And then she drops a brief and modern curtsy,
And glides away, assured she never hurts ye.

Such are Byron's illusions—thoroughly to be despised, but never
to be forsaken. Stanza 63 is perhaps especially remarkable. Here

Byron closes out this part of his digression and appears to recover some of his initial detachment. In reality, the pose has only been further unmasked and the reader is left to wonder at the depth and persistence of Byron's self-deceptions.

This is the drama of Romantic poetry where one becomes what one beholds, where education must be suffered through, where every poet is an Apollyon who must be pierced with his own weapon. In the splendid stanzas which culminate Canto XI, Byron raises up a nostalgic series of Pictures from the Gone World of 1814:

76

"Where is the world," cries Young, "at *eighty*? Where
The world in which a man was born?" Alas!
Where is the world of eight *years* past? '*Twas there*—
I look for it—'tis gone, a Globe of Glass!
Cracked, shivered, vanished, scarcely gazed on, ere
A silent change dissolves the glittering mass.
Statesmen, chiefs, orators, queens, patriots, kings,
And dandies, all are gone on the wind's wings.

77

Where is Napoleon the Grand? God knows:
Where little Castlereagh? The devil can tell:
Where Grattan, Curran, Sheridan, all those
Who bound the bar or senate in their spell?
Where is the unhappy Queen, with all her woes?
And where the Daughter, whom the Isle loved well?
Where are those martyred Saints the Five per Cents?
And where—oh where the devil are the Rents!

78

Where's Brummell? Dished. Where's Long Pole Wellesley?
Diddled.
Where's Whitbread? Romilly? Where's George the Third?
Where is his will? (That's not so soon unriddled.)

And where is "Fum" the Fourth, our "royal bird"?
Gone down it seems to Scotland to be fiddled
Unto by Sawney's violin, we have heard:
"Caw me, caw thee"—for six months hath been hatching,
This scene of royal itch and loyal scratching.

What, we wonder, is Byron doing in this lament over the passage of such a world, whose triviality he sees perfectly well? Is this what we should expect from the Pilgrim of Eternity? Is this the place, as Heine might say, to lament the Regency?

The answer, of course, as we are all aware, is yes. This is the place, and this is precisely what we must expect, for the pilgrim shuffles along through this passage as surely as he marched across Italy. The pathos, even the tragedy, of his progress is perhaps more profound here in *Don Juan* than it was in *Childe Harold's Pilgrimage.* For here the whole truth emerges with an almost unbearable clarity: that whenever Byron says "I have not loved the world, nor the world me" (*Childe Harold* III, st. 113) he is uttering a desperate and piteous lie. The truth is that he has loved it much too long and far too well, and that in this love his illusions (which are part of his loves) have always been threatened with collapse. Byron's poetry is born in the conflict of love and illusion, in the contradictions which are a necessary part of that conflict.

Here at the end of Canto XI the pity of those contradictions approaches a tragic level because here we see that Byron's illusion of detachment is utterly imaginary.

79

Where is Lord This? And where my Lady That?
The Honourable Mistresses and Misses?
Some laid aside like an old opera hat,
  Married, unmarried, and remarried: (this is
An evolution oft performed of late).
  Where are the Dublin shouts—and London hisses?
Where are the Grenvilles? Turned as usual. Where
My friends the Whigs? Exactly where they were.

80

Where are the Lady Carolines and Franceses?
 Divorced or doing thereanent. Ye annals
So brilliant, where the list of routs and dances is,—
 Thou Morning Post, sole record of the pannels
Broken in carriages, and all the phantasies
 Of fashion,—say what streams now fill those channels?
Some die, some fly, some languish on the Continent,
Because the times have hardly left them *one* tenant.

He has triumphed over nothing, been superior to nothing—not even to that "Globe of Glass" the Regency, or all those "Lady Carolines and Franceses." Rather, Byron has been in love and he has loved what vanishes. Here at the outset of the final movement of *Don Juan*, he parades before us the touching tableau of his emotional commitments, and all those butterflies he has loved and hated, sought and scorned. Their images arrest our attention and focus our sense of the contradictions defined in this poetry.

What is easiest to miss in this passage, however, is Byron's greatest love of all, the deep truth to which he has been committed but which has always remained imageless in his, as in all, Romantic poetry. That is to say, what we can miss are Byron's Romantic illusions, the ideas and the ideologies which lead him into a disclosure of his world's contradictions by tempting him to believe that they can be transcended in imaginative thought, "our last and only place/ Of refuge" (*Childe Harold* IV, st. 127). In the end Byron's poetry discovers what all Romantic poems repeatedly discover: that there is no place of refuge, not in desire, not in the mind, not in imagination. Man is in love and loves what vanishes, and this includes—finally, tragically—even his necessary angels.

Conclusion

Near the beginning of *The Romantic School* Heine delivers a mordant pronouncement on the historical fate of past cultures when they undergo a serious critical assessment. "Every epoch is a sphinx," Heine says, "that plunges into the abyss as soon as its riddle has been solved" (132). Implicit in this statement is a view which has been taken by many as a threat to the trans-historical power of art and poetry. Heine's remark asserts that the fate of past cultures is not merely a physical destruction, but spiritual and intellectual ruin as well. Time and the world's force will obliterate the material being of the past; the mind and its historical consciousness will take care of what remains. All human culture is bound for the abyss.

Romantic and post-Romantic art is peculiarly sensitive to this threat to its spiritual being—which is why so much of this art determines to assert its spiritual and absolutist claims. Romantic work produces (or affects to produce) Poems on Affairs of Soul, not at all *Poems on Affairs of State*. To follow Heine's line of criticism, then, might seem at best a perverse refusal to take Romantic works on their own terms, and at worst a dangerous undermining maneuver which puts at risk the very works one has set out to elucidate.

I have taken this course, however, precisely because I wish to face again, in a critical medium, the historical challenge which Romantic poetry originally had to face in art. Indeed, Heine's critique of Romanticism seems to me as impressive as it is because he understood at once the force and the limit of the historical challenge. His great essay lays Romanticism under the threat of historical backwardness, it is true, but in doing so it also finds a means for saving the valuable products of Romantic culture from obsolescence.

I would like to close this book by recalling, in a general way, the nature of Heine's critical achievement. I shall do so by way of a short digressive consideration of another critic of eminence, our contemporary, whose work first explained for me the method and significance of Heine's criticism.

Galvano della Volpe's important *Critica del Gusto*[1] does not mention Heine, yet the book brings a self-conscious and philosophical approach to bear on many of the same topics which Heine only treats in a practical and intuitive way. The book is an argument for a critical method which Della Volpe calls "dialectical paraphrase." The demonstration is complex and often extremely difficult, but the essential procedure can be summed up, without (I hope) too much distortion, as follows.

Della Volpe begins by showing the historical discreteness of particular poems. A series of practical analyses of specific poetical works taken from various cultures and periods (the examples range from Sophocles to Eliot and Mayakovsky) show that "each of them presupposes and contains within its structure as a poetically signifying organism a quite different historical rationale and quite different ideological and cultural. . .conditions from those of our own time" (30). Della Volpe does not say as much, but the force of his argument depends upon his decision to begin the analysis with texts that stand at a severe historical remove from the present, and to shift only gradually into a consideration of twentieth-century texts. This maneuver establishes his criticism in a permanent condition of historical dialectic with respect to his texts, on the one hand, and his readers on the other.

The maneuver equally establishes ideology and its various concrete forms at the center of his study. For Della Volpe, poetical works are organic structures which "reflect" the time- and place-specific characteristics of certain social forms and experiences: "Each of these poetic organisms refers back. . .to conditions which are. . .historical, social, and by implication economic." As the bearers of "structural values and poetic meanings," however, poems necessarily establish these material conditions, within the poetical text itself, as "*congruent* and *coherent* with the content-values of the work" (182). Herein lies what he calls "the *intellectual* nature of poetry," which is equally the basis for "the methodological criterion of the *dialectical paraphrase*" (the positive pole of his criticism), and the attack upon various contemporary schools of literary thought (the negative pole of his criticism). His attack on certain dominant trends of Marxist aesthetics is particularly important in this connection. "It is a flagrant contradiction," he says, "to emphasize [the power of poetry]'to reflect a society and its ideology' and still believe in art, as many self-styled Marxist philosophers persist in doing, as intuitive knowledge or knowledge 'through images', in abstract antithesis to science, understood as knowledge 'through concepts'" (183).

Della Volpe's method of dialectical paraphrase is his critical method for saving poetry from the ruins of historical change and cultural transformation. It entails, first, the articulation, via historical methods, of "the philosophical or sociological '*equivalent*' of the poetic thought." When this has been done the critic goes on to set this equivalent in a dialectical relation with the poetic text in order to reveal the equivalent as "an *uncritical paraphrase*, in other words the *degradation* of [the specifically poetical] thought . . . a *hybrid thought*, neither poetic nor scientific, neither polysemic nor univocal" (194). This critical operation provides a graphic demonstration of how ideology is a vital functioning element in poetical works. At the same time, it does not abstract the ideological elements from the poetry. The critical procedure is an heuristic act of abstraction which is precisely designed to avoid reducing poems to abstractions, either by freezing them into formal structures, or by reducing them to (good or bad) ideas:

> literary analysis based on the dialectical, and therefore critical, paraphrase of poetic texts is in a position to avoid both formalism and fixation on content. . . . Firstly, once we can perceive the true nature of the so-called philosophical or sociological or historical equivalent of the poetic text, namely that it is a paraphrase (though an uncritical one) of the. . .'content' in question, and thereby a reduction of it. . .then a comparison will necessarily be instituted between this paraphrase and the poetic thought or 'content' which it paraphrases. Why? Because a comparison of this sort is dictated, unavoidably, by a *quid* which separates, or at any rate distinguishes, the poetic thought from its paraphrase; the awareness of this distinguishing *quid* is precisely the beginning of taste, without it there is no literary criticism worthy of the name. (193)

Della Volpe illustrates his point by calling Lukács to task for his accurate but misguided critique of *Madame Bovary*:

We may note the failure of Lukács to understand *Madame Bovary*, a novel which he accuses of descriptivism for its own sake, in short, formalism. The faults of Lukács's fixation with content are exemplified when he complains that Flaubert tried to remedy the 'immobility', the 'empty and dispirited greyness' of his mediocre heroes by 'purely artistic and technical means' (*sic*). This attempt was 'bound to fail' because the 'mediocrity of the average man derives from the fact that the *social antinomies* which objectively determine his existence do not attain their highest degree of tension in him; on the contrary, they are obfuscated and attain a superficial equilibrium'. Flaubert is here condemned for giving artistic life to a social content which is not, for example, that of Zola and does not happen to square with the social ideas of his sociologist critic. But Lukács forgets how much he still owes Flaubert. What he owes him is all the poetic *truth* possessed by that 'mediocre pair', as Flaubert called them, in whom precisely everything, including first and foremost their consciousness of social antinomies, is shown to be *superficial*. (189)

Della Volpe's critical method rescues the literary work as much from the danger of a formalist reduction as from the threat of historical relativity. The method of dialectical paraphrase applies a kind of litmus paper test to the work, revealing thereby where and how the ideological elements operate. The paraphrase is an "abstraction," but because it is recognized to be an uncritical reduction of the work's content—an abstract or shadow-content, as it were—the literary analyst can *apply* it to the work in a useful and entirely critical way. The abstract "equivalent" of the work's ideological content throws the latter into relief. In addition, this shadow-content provides a standard which enables us to distinguish between the poetical and the historical existence of certain specific ideological forms. Precisely this kind of distinction Lukács does not make, according to Della Volpe: that is to say, Lukács's judgment upon *Madame Bovary* misses the point because it has not been able to distinguish between how ideology appears in a work of art, on the one hand, and how it operates in the world which that work of art "reflects," on the other. Lukács is able to distinguish the precise form of the Flaubertian "superficiality" partly because he has already been shown its forms in the world of *Madame Bovary*.

Della Volpe's theory of criticism has much in common with Heine's practice. Heine's contemptuous polemical assault upon German Romanticism, epitomized in his *ad hominem* attack upon Schlegel, his teacher, is manifestly "unfair" and "distorted." Were we to take this criticism *literally*—were we to read it as a "true" representation of either German Romanticism or its specific works—we would be missing the point of Heine's essay. Heine's critique is what Della Volpe calls an "equivalent" or "dialectical paraphrase." Its distortions and exaggerated polemics establish a *quid* between the reader and Heine's topic. The procedure gives the reader a standard of measurement and understanding; and it gives to Heine as well the chance to turn dialectically on his own subjects. That he seizes this opportunity is plain from what actually takes place in the essay: that is to say, Heine implicitly acknowledges the heuristic character of his own polemical distortions when he sets forth the various (specific) achievements of the German Romantics. The perpetual play of his witty, often outrageous prose allows him to draw distinctions between the illusions of Romantic Ideology and the illusions of a Romantic Art. The former are subject to the Critique of the Mind, which unriddles their secrets in order precisely to cast them into the abyss of history. The latter, however, are subject only to the Critique of Taste, which is benevolent and conservative, and which saves the appearances of poetry—including its ideological apparitions—from an ideological appropriation.

To the extent that Heine's essay is a critical (rather than an artistic) work, its own polemical distortions lay it open to the critique of the actual poetical works it presumes to judge. Everything of art that we inherit has this power to pass judgment upon the (necessarily partial and distorted) ideas and attitudes of the present, because the work of art is always discrete, finished (formally), and not abstract. Practical thought, on the other hand, is necessarily generalized, uncompleted, and abstract. Heine's essay, however, actively generates and responds to its own polemical moves, so that the practise of the essay institutes a critique on itself. To the extent that this takes place, the essay functions toward its own ideas as a work of art. The essay judges and criticizes its own critical positions.

This aspect of the essay seems to me one of its most important features so far as the literary critic is concerned, for it reminds us that if the critic lays art under the microscope, a mordant eye returns his quizzing gaze.[2] The greatness of Heine's essay is that it so often pursues an encounter with that searching poetic eye. Heine therefore read Uhland's poems in 1833 to his profit, and the rhetorical question he then put to his audience—"Is this the place to read Uhland's poems?"—might as well be asked now, of the academy, in an alternative form: "Is this the place to read Heine's essay?" The answer Heine looked to have then is exactly the same as what we should look to have now.

Afterword:

The German Ideology Once Again

My Conclusion to this book was written against the background of the post-New Critical academic situation,[1] and especially in the context of the work on ideology and art which has been developed recently by Althusser, Macherey, and Eagleton. The central texts are Macherey's *A Theory of Literary Production*, originally published in 1966; Althusser's great essay "Ideology and Ideological State Apparatuses," which he wrote early in 1969; and Eagleton's influential book *Criticism and Ideology*, published in 1976. These critics have been important in the contemporary scene of literary criticism because their interpretative methods—consciously antithetical to the traditional lines of literary interpretation as these have come down to us—have had a substantial impact on the current view (and views) of academic criticism. To understand the antithesis represented by these works we shall first have to reconsider briefly *The German Ideology* since Marx's work provides these contemporary commentators with their point of departure.[2]

The German Ideology is a brilliantly satirical critique of the dominant "infantile disorder" of Marx's day, that is, of left-wing Hegelian criticism. Feuerbach, Bauer, Stirner, and—to a lesser extent—Strauss had represented themselves and their work in a revolutionary guise. These men, the specifically *German* ideologues, aimed to "liberate" mankind "from the rule of concepts" (23). They launched an attack upon the dominion of various bourgeois ideologies in order to free the mind from a "false consciousness" of the human condition.

Marx's and Engels' purpose in their work is to expose the illusory character of the entire program of the radical Hegelians:

> These innocent and child-like fancies are the kernel of the modern Young-Hegelian philosophy, which not only is received by the German public with horror and awe, but is announced by our *philosophic heroes* with the solemn consciousness of its world-shattering danger and criminal ruthlessness. The first volume of the present publication has the air of uncloaking these sheep, who

take themselves and are taken for wolves; of showing
that their bleating merely imitates in a philosophic form
the conceptions of the German middle class; that the
boasting of these philosophic commentators only mirrors the wretchedness of the real conditions in Germany. (23)

In other words, Marx is saying that the attack on bourgeois
ideology by the German ideologists is itself enmeshed in a network of illusions. Like the radical Hegelians he is attacking,
Marx agrees that bourgeois society is held in thrall to certain
reactionary and illusive ideas. But Marx attacks the German
ideologues because their critique of society is made from a
purely theoretical and abstract position. The illusion in the
specifically *German* form of bourgeois ideology is that a critique
of ideology can be made in the realm of ideas. The illusion is
not merely that one set of (presumptively) correct ideas can
"liberate" people from their subjection to other "truly illusive"
ideas; even more, the illusion is that a critique of ideology can
be launched from, and grounded in, conceptual space. That
"innocent and child-like" notion *is* The German Ideology:

We shall, of course, not take the trouble to explain to
our wise philosophers that the "liberation" of "man" is
not advanced a single step by reducing philosophy,
theology, substance and all the rubbish to "self-
consciousness" and by liberating "man" from the domi-
nation of these phrases, which have never held him in
thrall. Nor shall we explain to them that it is possible to
achieve real liberation only in the real world and by real
means, that slavery cannot be abolished without the
steam-engine and the mule jenny, serfdom cannot be
abolished without improved agriculture, and that, in
general, people cannot be liberated as long as they are
unable to obtain food and drink, housing and clothing
in adequate quality and quantity. "Liberation" is a historical and not a mental act, and it is brought about by
historical   conditions,   the   [level]   of   industry,
com[merce], [agri]culture, [intercourse. . .] then subse-
quently, in accordance with the different stages of their
development, [they make up] the nonsense of substance,
subject, self-consciousness and pure criticism, as well as
religious and theological nonsense, and later they get rid

of it again when their development is sufficiently advanced. In Germany, a country where only a trivial historical development is taking place, these mental developments, these glorified and ineffective trivialities, naturally serve as a substitute for the lack of historical development, and they take root and have to be combated. (38)

It is in the context of Marx's (rather contemptuous) dismissal of German Ideology that we have to consider the recent work of Althusser, Macherey, and Eagleton. In 1966, apparently under the influence of Macherey's work on Lenin and Tolstoy, Althusser wrote: "*I do not rank real art among the ideologies.*"[3] By this statement Althusser meant to align art and (what he calls) "scientific knowledge" as the two types of human activity which are not subject to the imaginary dislocations of ideological knowledge. For Althusser—and, in this respect, he speaks for virtually all English, West European, and American Marxist thinkers—ideology is "false consciousness," or (more particularly) the system of structures and concrete apparatuses which generate and maintain an "imaginary representation of the real world" (154). Like scientific knowledge, however, art—according to this view of the matter—at once escapes a subjection to ideology and preserves itself as a weapon for exposing the existence, the precise character, and the domain of particular ideologies (and, sometimes, of ideology in general).

Macherey's book shares all of these Althusserian positions, but it goes on to specify how art escapes, and even attacks, the ideological realities which it represents. The operative term in Macherey's analysis is "absence."

Between the ideology and the book which expresses it, something has happened; the distance between them is not the product of some abstract decorum. Even though ideology itself always sounds solid, copious, it begins to speak of its *own absence* because of its presence in the novel, its visible and determinate form. By means of the text it becomes possible to escape from the domain of spontaneous ideology, to escape from the false consciousness of self, of history, and of time. The text constructs a determinate image of the ideological, revealing it as an object rather than living it from within as though it were an inner conscience; the text explores ideology (just as Balzac explores the Paris of the *Comèdie humaine, for instance), puts it to the test of the written word, the test of that watchful gaze in which all subjectivity is captured* crystallised in objective form. The spontaneous ideology in which men live (it is not produced spontaneously, although men believe that they acquire it spontaneously) is not simply reflected by the mirror of the book; ideology is broken, and turned inside out in so far as it is transformed in the text from being a state of consciousness. Art, or at least literature, because it naturally scorns the credulous view of the world, establishes myth and illusion as *visible objects*. (132-3)

A passage like this indicates the close affinity which exists between Macherey and the Frankfurt School, and in particular with Adorno's idea that art is the negative knowledge of reality. We must keep this relationship in mind if we mean to fill out our sense of the relationship of Macherey's work to the most influential recent trends in Western Marxist thought about art and literature.

A dual weakness haunts this view of art and ideology, however, and it reflects the persistent hold which certain types of Romantic idealism have even in the Marxian wings of the academy. Macherey and Althusser set poetry apart from ideology because they identify the latter with false consciousness and historical limits. Because poetry and art appear to transcend such limits, they are not ranked among the ideologies. This is clearly a rationalist conclusion in a rationalist form of thought. The view is belied in the actual facts of the poems from the past which we read, as well as in the poems of the present which are being written. Furthermore, it is a view which betrays a corresponding idealization of criticism, and in particular of the criticism practiced by Macherey and Althusser themselves.[4]

Let me begin with the poems and their relation to ideology. As has been argued in the course of the previous study, and as Marx himself said in *The German Ideology*, works of art—depending as they do upon their special circumstances of production and of reproduction—will represent themselves, or be made to represent through our criticism, the widest possible variety of ideological positions. Furthermore, the ideology of a given work (say, *Aurora Leigh*) will assume various specific forms, and these will be ranged at different points on a scale of social consciousness. These ideological forms can be studied within the confines of the poem or they can be separated from the poem and examined in their own right, formally or historically. A good deal of Elizabeth Barrett Browning's poem still seems ideologically advanced to this day because our own cultures have not yet settled accounts with certain of the most basic rights of women. From an historical point of view, the ideological forms enmeshed within the poem will be seen to have changed their import over time. Poetry, however, saves those ideas and attitudes intact by arresting them forever in expressive forms which will always be, from the poem's original point of view, historically and socially particular. For the reader (any reader) of *Aurora Leigh*, the set of ideological formations imbedded in the poem at its historical inception will always remain part of the work's fixed dialectical pole with which the moving pole of the reader interacts. Both poles are historically specific, the one fixed in time and place, the other moving in the field which we now call the work's reception history.

For this reason we must say that a poem's formal and substantive components, whether retrograde or advanced, preserve their original specificity. If they did not do so the poem would lose all its concrete force, all its specific human contours, as Della Volpe (for one) has so well shown.[5]

Althusser's position is implicitly contradicted in his own celebrated essay on Ideological State Apparatuses, a work that also provides the ground for a more critical view of the forms and practice of criticism itself, including Marxist criticism. Althusser's gripping argument shows that all ideological phenomena, including poetry, are produced and reproduced within some concrete historical apparatus. Poetry is written, and read, within the determinate limits of specific social structures. This crucial fact tends to be ignored by all the literary critics in the tradition I am sketching. The neglect occurs not merely with respect to poetry as it has been culturally produced (i.e., poetry as a written phenomenon), but even more crucially with respect to poetry as it has been *re*produced (i.e., poetry as an object of reading and study). Great poetry is not written out of the conceptual space of a "German Ideology," and neither does criticism occur in such a space. Both take place within concrete and specific Ideological State Apparatuses. As far as modern criticism is concerned, this means that the theory and practise of criticism reflect the authority of the western university's complex ideological structures.

Too much Western Marxist literary criticism fails to take account of its own investment in the Ideological State Apparatuses which we operate within—indeed, which we all serve. Reading and studying poetry (reproducing it), just as much as writing it (producing it), is a tendentious affair, whether we are conscious of that fact or not. The problem is that many Marxist critics do not recognize, or take account of, the specific ideological determinants of their own work. *A Theory of Literary Production*, like Eagleton's *Criticism and Ideology*, seems to transcend not merely its subject but its own originating environment (something which the art criticism of John Berger does not do). But this seeming *is* an illusion, and a concrete instance of a false consciousness that must be overcome. To argue art's ideological disengagement merely reifies that most fundamental of all bourgeois aesthetic concepts: that the essence of poetry is to transcend, and to make the reader transcend, concrete spatial and temporal circumstances. Such a view of poetry and art develops its own necessary critical method and theory, that is to say, one which speaks of poetry and art from the cool regions of mental disinterestedness. Reading many contemporary Marxist critics one is often reminded of Marx's eleventh thesis on Feuerbach.

Though I have—correctly, I believe—associated the work of Adorno, Althusser, Macherey, and Eagleton, I must point out that Eagleton's work is by far the most advanced, from a theoretical point of view. His critique of Althusser and Macherey is trenchant in many respects, not least because he is well aware that ideology operates historically, and hence that it appears in different forms and degrees of illusiveness. When Eagleton says that "some ideologies, and levels of ideology, are more false than others" (69), he follows Marx (and departs from his European mentors), for in *The German Ideology* Marx took pains to emphasize the special, "local" (38) character of the German Ideology, and to distinguish it from (for example) French and English ideological formations (55).

Furthermore, when Eagleton seeks to define the special type of ideological formation which is literature—when he attacks

Macherey for suggesting that literature is a *vehicle* for ideologies rather than an ideological form *per se*—he has made a truly signal advance in theoretical understanding.[6]

Nevertheless, Eagleton's arguments themselves contribute to that fetishization of art which is so characteristic of Western culture. The sure sign of this is Eagleton's constant resort to the term "text" when he speaks of literary works. For Eagleton, "text" and "work of art" are synonymous terms.

Such an idea is an illusion, however, as even a few moments of critical reflection will show. Submitting to that illusion has two immediate consequences: first, the literary work of art is fetishized—frozen, immobilized, abstracted—into an arrangement of words; and second, the critic comes to imagine himself as removed from the works he studies, analytically detached from the "text." For a Marxist critic, this set of related illusions permits him to imagine that his own criticism is uncontaminated either by the text's false consciousness or by the Ideological Apparatuses in which his criticism is carried on.

It is in this general context that we can see the special relevance which *The German Ideology* has for modern Marxist criticism: for the latter is, in many ways, a parodic version of the sort of left-wing Hegelianism which Marx was attacking in his book. The whole thrust of *The German Ideology* is to bring critique out of the realms of consciousness (out of "German" ideological space) and return it to the world of praxis. No criticism, not even literary criticism, can invoke a conceptual privilege for its activity. Least of all can it privilege the activities of critical consciousness.

Consequently, Marx's indictment of the radical Hegelians of his own day carries an application and a warning for our own:

> It has not occurred to any one of these philosophers to inquire into the connection of German philosophy with German reality, the connection of their criticism with their own material surroundings. (30)

Literary criticism today is practiced under the aegis of very particular sorts of Ideological State Apparatuses, and no adequate criticism can occur which does not force itself to take such conditions into account. In part this will mean that criticism must analyze, self-critically, the effect which those apparatuses have in shaping, and distorting, our critical activities. Such an analysis presupposes an historical inquiry into how the works we inherit have been reproduced in the past, that is to say, an analysis of the critical history of the works of literature which we are currently reproducing in our age. Furthermore, these analyses must continually translate themselves into those practical projects which address themselves to the fundamental issue: what is the function of criticism at the present time?

Criticism is historical not simply by explaining the "texts" we read in terms of the past historical contexts which penetrate them. Such a criticism must remain as fruitless and arid as any type of formal or structural or thematic criticism so long as it does not make equally explicit, first, the dialectical relation of the analyzed "texts" to present interests and concerns; and second, the immediate and projected ideological involvements of the criticism, critical theory, and reading we practice, study, and promote.

Works of literature neither produce nor reproduce themselves; only texts do that, which is merely to say that the idea of literature-as-text fetishizes works of art into passive objects, the consumer goods of a capitalized world. To return poetry to a human form—to see that what we read and study are poetic *works* produced and reproduced by numbers of specific men and women—is perhaps the most imperative task now facing the world of literary criticism. That purpose will only be fulfilled when literary critics, especially Marxist critics, cease reproducing texts and begin *re*producing literary works of art.

Notes

INTRODUCTION

1. See "Presentation II," in *Aesthetics and Politics*, Afterword by Frederick Jameson (London, 1977), 60-85.

2. I suppose it does not need to be said, at this late hour, that these levels interpenetrate with each other at all points. We distinguish the levels for purposes of analysis.

3. *The Statesman's Manual*, in S. T. Coleridge, *Lay Sermons*, ed. R. J. White (Princeton, 1972), 22-3.

4. *Ibid.*, 23-4.

5. *Ibid.*, 28.

6. *Ibid.*, 17-18.

7. *The Table Talk and Omniana of S.T. Coleridge*, ed. T. Ashe (London, 1923), 138-9 (entry for 12 Sept. 1831). For a more detailed discussion of Coleridge's views on these matters see my "The Meaning of the Ancient Mariner," *Critical Inquiry* 8 (Autumn, 1981), 35-67, and Elinor Shaffer's important study *'Kubla Khan' and the Fall of Jerusalem* (Cambridge, 1975).

8. I have borrowed the Scott and Napoleon quotations from Raymond Williams' discussion of ideology in *Keywords* (Oxford, 1976), 126-7. For a good general introduction to the early history of the concept of ideology see Emmet Kennedy," 'Ideology' from Destutt de Tracy to Marx," *Journal of the History of Ideas* 40 (July-Sept., 1979), 353-68.

9. *The German Ideology*, in Karl Marx and Frederick Engels, *The Collected Works* II (New York, 1976), 60.

10. Engels, letter to Franz Mehring, 14 July 1893, in *Marx. Engels. On Art and Literature* (Moscow, 1976), 65.

11. *The German Ideology*, 61-2.

12. Engels, *Ludwig Feuerbach*, ed. C. P. Dutt (New York, 1941), 56.

13. For a more extended theoretical discussion of this point see below, Conclusion.

14. See below part II, n. 7, and the Afterword, "The German Ideology Once Again."

PART I

1. See A. O. Lovejoy's "On the Discrimination of Romanticisms," *PMLA* 39 (1924), 229-53; and Réne Wellek, "The Concept of Romanticism in Literary Scholarship," *Comparative Literature* 1 (1949), 1-23, 147-72. Wellek's essay is reprinted in his *Concepts of Criticism* (New Haven, Conn., 1963), 128-98, and it is the latter text I shall be citing below. The concepts of "intrinsic" and "historical" Romanticism are employed by Jacques Barzun in *Classic, Romantic, and Modern* (Boston, 1961). The scholarly literature on the subject of Romanticism is extensive, and in my presentation I synthesize and trace out the chief

lines of thought on the subject as it has developed from the 1790s to the present. At all points the center of interest is English Romanticism and the investigations thereof. For a good recent survey of Romanticism and the scholarly history of its investigations see the series of essays printed in *'Romantic' and Its Cognates: The European History of a Word*, ed. Hans Eichner (Toronto, 1972); see also Eichner's interesting essay "The Rise of Modern Science and the Genesis of Romanticism," *PMLA* 97 (Jan., 1982), 8-30.

2. Wellek, *ibid.*, 161.

3. Vol. 7 no. 4 (Autumn, 1976). The quotations in this paragraph are from Ruoff's introduction, 289 and 290.

4. The essay appears in *Jane Austen in a Social Context*, ed. David Monaghan (Totowa, N.J., 1981), 9-27.

5. Ruoff, *ibid.*, 290.

6. Anne Mellor, *English Romantic Irony* (Cambridge, Mass., 1980), vii.

7. *Ibid.*, 5.

8. *Ibid.*

9. *The Compass of Irony* (London, 1969); see especially 194-9 and 242-5.

10. Mellor, vii. I should note here the continuity which exists between Mellor's view and Wellek's. Indeed, Wellek explicitly excludes "nihilism, 'alienation' from our definition of Romanticism" ("Romanticism Re-Examined," in *Concepts of Criticism*, 200). Once again the problem centers in Byron and what Peckham called "Negative Romanticism." Wellek rightly dismisses this "purely verbal solution" (*ibid.*) to the problem represented by Romantic "nihilism," but one must surely find his own definitional solution equally unsatisfactory.

11. Soren Kierkegaard, *The Concept of Irony*, trans. Lee M. Capel (London, 1966).

12. Praz, *The Romantic Agony* 2d ed. (N.Y., 1950), 14-15.

13. Romantic works are rarely characterized in this way anymore, possibly because such terms are not thought to be likely to attract an audience to the importance of Romanticism. Readers like to think that literary works will benefit their lives, and nihilistic works do not seem, at first glance, to serve that purpose.

14. M. H. Abrams, "English Romanticism: The Spirit of the Age," in *Romanticism Reconsidered*, ed. Northrop Frye (N.Y., 1963), 53.

15. *Ibid.*, 55.

16. *Ibid.*, 57-9.

17. See *The Ringers in the Tower* (Chicago, 1971), 13-36, where the essay is reprinted.

18. Abrams is merely repeating here what Wordsworth had said throughout *The Prelude*.

19. See Frank E. Manuel, *The Eighteenth Century Confronts the Gods* (Cambridge, Mass., 1959), and A. J. Kuhn, "English Deism and the Development of Romantic Mythological Syncretism," *PMLA* 71 (1956), 1094-1116.

20. J. Robert Barth, *The Symbolic Imagination: Coleridge and the Romantic Tradition* (Princeton, 1977), 127.

21. Alison G. Sulloway, "Emma Woodhouse and *A Vindication of the Rights of Woman*," *The Wordsworth Circle*, 320.

22. *The Great Chain of Being* (Cambridge, Mass., 1936), chap. 10, "Romanticism and the Principle of Plenitude."

23. Wellek, 182.

24. *Biographia Literaria*, chap. 14.

25. See below, chap. 5.

26. All quotations from Heine's *Die romantische Schule* are taken from *Heinrich Heine. Selected Works*, ed. Helen Mustard (N.Y., 1963). Page references are given in the text. For the German text the reader should consult the critical edition edited by Renate Franke, *Heines Werke. Säkularausgabe Band 8* (Berlin, 1972).

27. A polemic for a past form of thought or feeling is in fact a general obligation of criticism, for it is from the past that we draw our critical measurements of and in the present. Nevertheless, the choice of a critical measure of present illusions must be carefully done, and even more carefully applied. Too often scholarship allows itself to be used as the apologist for the most retrograde ideologies of the present—to express and confirm, through the words of the great artists of the past, the debased attitudes of the contemporary consciousness industries. In short, to produce criticism in a bad faith.

28. Peckham, "On Romanticism: Introduction," *Studies in Romanticism* 9 (1970), 218.

29. The clearest presentation of this subject is in Allan Rodway, *The Romantic Conflict* (London, 1963).

30. I quote from Blake's *The Marriage of Heaven and Hell* earlier in the paragraph, and from Byron's "Dedication" to *Don Juan* at the end.

31. Geoffrey Hartman, "Romanticism and Anti-Selfconsciousness," in *Beyond Formalism* (New Haven, Conn., 1970), 302-3.

32. Peckham, 218.

33. *Table Talk*, 136-9.

34. *Ibid.*, 230.

35. *Ibid.*, 211.

36. *Ibid.*, 212.

37. "Introduction to the Philosophy of Art," in *Hegel. Selections*, ed. and trans. J. Loewenberg (N.Y., 1929), 321-2. The following quotations are all taken from this translation of Hegel's Preface to his *Vorlesungen über die Aesthetik*, and page numbers are given in the text.

38. See above, Introduction.

39. For a nice discussion of Coleridge's works and their relation to fragmentariness see Thomas McFarland, *Romanticism and the Forms of Ruin* (Princeton, 1981). For a synthetic analysis of Romantic poetic forms and the convention of fragment poetry see the brilliant thesis of Marjorie Levinson, *The Romantic Fragment Poem: A Critical Study* (Ph.D. thesis, U. of Chicago, 1978).

40. See Franke, *Heines Werke, op. cit.*, 114n.

PART II

1. L. J. Swingle, "On Reading Romantic Poetry," *PMLA* 86 (1971), 974. Further references to this essay will be given in the text.

2. See, for example, Carl Woodring's comments on the piece in the *Keats-Shelley Journal* 30 (1981), 192.

3. See above, chap. 2

4. King's relation to the poem is conveniently discussed in Maynard Mack's edition of *An Essay on Man* (London, 1950), xxvii-xxix.

5. One should note here, however, that although Byron does not seek to disguise his ideological commitments, he is not always reliably self-conscious about them. See below, chap. 14.

6. I take my text from *The Poems of Sir Philip Sidney*, ed. William A. Ringler (Oxford, 1962), 161-2.

7. It is Althusser who said that art was not among the ideologies; see Louis Althusser, *Lenin and Philosophy* (London, 1971), 203, and below, Afterword. For a typical formulation of the view that poetry deals with "universals" rather than with historical particulars see John Ellis, *The Theory of Literary Criticism: A Logical Analysis* (Berkeley, Ca., 1974).

8. Text from *Byron. The Complete Poetical Works*, ed. Jerome J. McGann (Oxford, 1981) II, 93. Unless otherwise noted, this will be the text for all quotations from Byron.

9. Text from *William Wordsworth. Poems*, ed. John O. Hayden (New York, 1977) I, 364. Unless otherwise noted, this will be the text for all quotations from Wordsworth.

10. *Shelley's Prose: The Trumpet of a Prophecy*, ed. David Lee Clark (Albuquerque, N.M., 1954), 83-4.

11. See *Religious Lyrics of the XIVth Century*, ed. Carleton Brown, 2d ed. (Oxford, 1957), 83-4.

12. Quotations from Donne are taken from *The Poems of John Donne*, ed. H.J.C. Grierson (Oxford, 1912).

13. The present discussion of Keats may be supplemented with my essay "Keats and the Historical Method in Literary Criticism," *Modern Language Notes* 94 (1979), 988-1032.

14. See *The Keats Circle. Letters and Papers 1816-1879*, ed. H. E. Rollins (Cambridge, Mass., 1965) II, 185.

15. My texts for this ballad, as well as for the Scott derivatives discussed below, are to be found in *The Complete Poetical Works of Sir Walter Scott*, ed. Horace E. Scudder (Cambridge, Mass., 1900), 32-7.

16. In a recent series of papers I have tried to demonstrate the practical methods that are involved in a critical project of this sort. See n. 13 above as well as "The Text, the Poem, and the Problem of Historical Method," *New Literary History* 12 (1981), 269-88; "The Meaning of the Ancient Mariner," *Critical Inquiry* 8 (Autumn, 1981), 35-67; "The Anachronism of George Crabbe," *English Literary History* 48 (1981), 555-72; "Christina Rossetti: A New Edition and a Revaluation," *Victorian Studies* 23 (Winter, 1980), 237-54; "Shall These Bones Live?" *Text* 1 (not yet published); and two essays which will be published shortly, "Tennyson and the Histories of Criticism" (to appear in *Review*) and "Textual and Bibliographical Studies and Their Meaning for Literary Criticism" (to appear in a collection of essays by various hands).

17. My text for this poem is James Butler's critical edition, *The Ruined Cottage and The Pedlar* (Ithaca, N.Y., 1979). The most comprehensive discussion of the poem can be found in Jonathan Wordsworth, *The Music of Humanity* (London, 1969).

18. *Ibid.*, 4.

19. Marjorie Levinson, "Insight and Oversight: A Reading of 'Tintern Abbey'," unpublished manuscript essay.

20. See Hans Magnus Enzensberger, *The Consciousness Industry: On Literature, Politics, and the Media* (N.Y., 1974).

21. Pierre Machery, *A Theory of Literary Production*, trans. Geoffrey Wall (London, 1978), 132.

PART III

1. See Coleridge's discussions of the differences between allegory and symbol in *The Statesman's Manual*, 29-31, and his

Lectures on Literature, in *Coleridge's Miscellaneous Criticism*, ed. T. M. Raysor (London, 1936), 99-103.

2. See E. H. Coleridge's edition of *Coleridge. Poetical Works* (Oxford, 1967 reprint), 589n. All quotations from Coleridge's poetry are taken from this edition.

3. W. J. Bate, *Coleridge* (N.Y., 1968), 178.

4. *Ibid.*, 179.

5. Harold Bloom, *The Visionary Company* (N.Y., 1961), 179.

6. By Geoffrey Hartman in his *Wordsworth's Poetry. 1787-1814* (New Haven, Conn., 1964), 8ff.

7. Norman Rudich, "'Kubla Khan', a Political Poem," *Romantisme* 8 (1974), 52-3.

8. The latter term is Louis Althusser's: see his great essay "Ideology and Ideological State Apparatuses," in *Lenin and Philosophy*, part 2, n. 7.

9. See John Carey's edition (Oxford, 1970), 38-43. The Brocken spectre is a variant form of a widely ramified (and fundamentally Romantic) set of images whose most typical form is the *ignis fatuus.*

10. See John Howard, "An Audience for *The Marriage of Heaven and Hell,*" *Blake Studies* 3 (1970), 19-52.

11. *Byron. Complete Poetical Works, op. cit.*, 91.

12. From *The Poems of Byron*, ed. P. E. More (Cambridge, Mass., 1905), 236.

13. Richard Holmes, *Shelley. The Pursuit* (London, 1974), 506.

14. The text here is from the edition of Donald H. Reiman and Sharon B. Powers, *Shelley's Poetry and Prose* (N.Y., 1977). Unless otherwise noted, all poetry will be quoted from this text.

15. *The Letters of Percy Bysshe Shelley*, ed. Frederick L. Jones (Oxford, 1964) II, 350.

16. *Ibid.*, 442.

17. Letter to Trusler, 23 Aug. 1799, in *The Poetry and Prose of William Blake*, ed. David V. Erdman (N.Y., 1965), 676-7.

18. *Byron's Letters and Journals*, ed. Leslie A. Marchand (Cambridge, Mass., 1974) III, 109; *The Letters of John Keats*, ed. H. E. Rollins (Cambridge, Mass., 1958) I, 185.

19. *Shelley's Prose*, 286.

20. *Letters* II, 176-7.

21. See above, part 2, n. 13.

22. From K. N. Cameron's "The Social Philosophy of Shelley,"

reprinted in *Shelley's Poetry and Prose*, 516.

23. Holmes, 678.

24. From the "Preface" to *Prometheus Unbound*.

25. The critical analysis of European philhellenism has yet to be made. But much excellent work has been produced describing this phenomenon. See Terence Spencer, *Fair Greece, Sad Relic* (London, 1954); William St. Clair, *That Greece Might Still Be Free* (London, 1972); and Harry Levin, *The Broken Column* (Cambridge, Mass., 1931).

26. *Don Juan. A Variorum Edition*, ed. T. G. Steffan and W. W. Pratt (Austin, Tex., 1957) III, 413-15. All citations of *Don Juan* are made to this edition.

27. *Shelley's Prose*, 293.

28. *The Poems of John Keats*, ed. Jack Stillinger (Cambridge, Mass., 1978), 372.

29. From my own point of view, this critical representation is most to be criticized in a book like my *Fiery Dust: Byron's Poetic Development* (Chicago, 1968); and see below, chap. 14.

CONCLUSION

1. This work is available in English as *Critique of Taste*, trans. Michael Caesar (London, 1978). I use the latter text and cite page references in parentheses in my text.

2. I was first made aware of how past poetry functions in this critical way toward the present by A. D. Hope in his *The Cave and the Spring* (Chicago, 1970).

AFTERWORD

1. For an excellent critical introduction to this topic see Frank Lentriccia, *After the New Criticism* (Chicago, 1980).

2. I use the text of *The German Ideology* cited above in the Introduction, n. 9. Page references here are supplied in the text.

3. See *Lenin and Philosophy*, 203.

4. The most trenchant critique to date of this Hegelian line of Marxist thought is E. P. Thompson, *The Poverty of Theory and Other Essays* (London, 1978), especially the long title piece. Another interesting criticism can be read in Tony Bennett, *Formalism and Marxism* (London, 1979), esp. 169-75. Bennett's critique is made from a theoretical vantage which is in fundamental sympathy with the Marxist line it is examining. Eagleton's work has itself always been wary of the Hegelian fault line in Marxist theory, and his most recent book represents, in my opinion, a most impressive theoretical position: see his *Walter Benjamin, or Towards a Revolutionary Criticism* (London, 1981).

5. In *Critique of Taste*; see esp. 24-45, 68-81.

6. Machery's more recent position aligns itself rather closely with Eagleton's. See Pierre Machery and Etienne Balibar, "Sur la littérature comme forme idéologique: quelques hypothèses marxistes," *Litterature* 13 (1974); twice translated into English, first in *The Oxford Literary Review* 3 (1978) and most recently in *Praxis* 5 (Part 1), 43-58 by James H. Kavanagh.

Index